MORMONISM

To my parents
James and Anastasia Bartley
to whom I owe so much.

Peter Bartley

MORMONISM

The Prophet, the Book and the Cult

VERITAS

First published 1989 by
Veritas Publications
7-8 Lower Abbey Street
Dublin 1

ISBN 1 85390 063 X

Cover design by Angela Shivnen
Typesetting by Printset & Design Ltd, Dublin
Printed in the Republic of Ireland by
Mount Salus Press

Acknowledgements

I owe a debt of gratitude to the Rev. Dr Maurice C. Burrell for agreeing to read that portion of the work comprising chapters 3, 4 and 5, the first to appear in typewritten form, and for his continued interest and support; to my daughters, Joanne and Colette, who helped in numerous small ways; and to the respective staffs of the Peterlee and Seaham branches of the Durham County Library, who were most helpful in supplying books otherwise difficult to obtain. I alone am responsible for any defects the work may contain.

Biblical quotations, in general, are taken from the *Revised Standard Version*, though it has been found necessary occasionally to quote from other translations. It should be remembered that Joseph Smith, the founder of Mormonism, knew only the *King James Version*.

Contents

Introduction

There can be few people who have never heard of the Mormon Church or, to give it its official title, the Church of Jesus Christ of Latter-day Saints. Mormon missionaries are active in almost 100 countries, and their doorstep style of presenting religion is well-known. Moreover, their clean-cut appearance, American accents and friendly manner have made them easily identifiable.

Mormonism has been around for a long time. Its origins date back to the beginning of the nineteenth century, making it much older than most other American fundamentalist sects. It became established in England as early as 1839. Its impact on American society has not been insignificant. Mormons are prominent in all the professions, and claim to have a higher literacy rate and better standard of education than any group of comparable size in America.[1]

It is probably true that Mormons are best-known for the more peripheral aspects of their faith. They are noted for their firm attachment to healthy living, which leads them to abstain from tobacco and alcohol, and even from tea and coffee. In these modern times we associate the age-old practice of tithing with the Mormons: the practice accounts for their Church's considerable wealth. And who has not heard of the famous Mormon Temple and Tabernacle Choir in Salt Lake City? In general, Mormons would seem to be exemplary Christians. Devout and industrious, they place strong emphasis on the importance of family life, and are renowned for their many charitable works.

While these traits are all relevant to our subject they leave a lot unsaid. We shall not return to them. This book is about fundamentals. It seeks to provide answers to the sort of questions any serious study of the movement would be likely to raise. How did Mormonism originate? What are its claims, its distinctive beliefs? What are we to make of the Book of Mormon? To what extent, if at all, can Mormonism be accounted a Christian movement? Is Mormonism reasonable? For no matter how commendable Mormonism appears in the personal witness of its adherents, these are questions of paramount interest that must be faced.

Chapter 1 relates the history of Joseph Smith, the founder of the sect, including the series of supernatural happenings he is said to have experienced, and the evidence advanced in its support. The early history of Mormonism, its successes and setbacks, is given attention. Smith's claims come under close scrutiny in chapter 2, in a critical and fair-minded spirit.

Part II of the book is taken up with the claims made for the bible of the movement, the Book of Mormon. It is held that in its original form the Book of Mormon was revealed to Joseph Smith by an angel, and that Smith translated it from the ancient language in which it was written. The book pretends to be the Old and New Testament of the ancient Americans. In Mormon eyes, it is equal in authority to the Holy Bible. Chapter 3 is given over to a candid presentation of the external evidence favoured by Mormons in their attempts to substantiate the genuineness of the book. Chapters 4 and 5 constitute a reply, in which the evidence of archaeology and ethnology is brought to bear on the subject. A chapter assessing the internal evidence for and against the Book of Mormon completes Part II of the book.

The allegation that Christianity failed at the outset and continued thereafter in an apostate condition, and the claim that Mormonism represents the restoration of Christianity in its pristine, uncorrupted state, will be examined in Part III, chapter 7. The final chapter is an assessment of Mormon doctrinal beliefs, drawing on the Mormon scriptures and the writings of Mormon theologians. Throughout, the book will be chiefly concerned with the Utah or Brighamite Mormons, as they form the largest and, through their doorstep proselytising, more familiar body of believers. However, the argument of the book, in the main, applies to all Mormons, insofar as all Mormons accept Joseph Smith as God's prophet and the Book of Mormon as the inspired Word of God and supplement to the Bible. Reference will be made to the dissenting group where differences of belief occur.

Anyone who has had any dealings with Mormons will have been impressed by their unshakeable faith in Joseph Smith, the man they believe was chosen by God to restore true religion to a world darkened by universal apostasy. Smith gave them their religion and their scriptures, and little of any great consequence has been added to Mormonism since his day.

PART I

The Prophet

1

The Mormon Story

Joseph Smith was born on 23 December 1805 in Sharon, Windsor County, Vermont, the son of Joseph Smith Snr and Lucy Mack Smith. When Joseph Jnr was ten years old the family moved to Palmyra, Ontario County, in the State of New York. Another move four years later took the family to Manchester, in the same county of Ontario, where the young Joseph remained until he reached manhood. During much of this time he worked alongside his father and brothers on the family farm.

Such are the bare, uncontroverted facts. To inquire further into the events of these years is to become embroiled in controversy. For what follows concerning the alleged supernatural happenings, we must have recourse to the Mormon version of events. This is to be found in the historical sketch which appears towards the end of the *Pearl of Great Price*, a compilation of Joseph Smith's writings which forms a part of the Mormon scriptures.

Smith's religious history began with an isolated incident said to have taken place when he was fourteen years of age. The western part of the State of New York was at that time gripped in a fever of extreme religious activity which caused it to become known as the 'Burned-over District'. In the revivalist camp meetings sect vied with sect for the attentions of the unaffiliated. Novelty in religion was not merely commonplace, it was almost demanded. Presbyterianism was the religion of Joseph Smith's family; but, though Joseph attended the camp meetings and inclined, as he tells us, to Methodism, he nevertheless remained aloof from all denominations.

Even so, religion interested and excited Joseph Smith, but the contradictory nature of the religious beliefs he heard expounded day in, day out disturbed his mind. Then, one day, he happened to be reading James 1:5 and came across the words:

> If any one of you lack wisdom,
> let him ask of God, that giveth
> to all men liberally, and upbraideth not;
> and it shall be given him.

Smith described the profound effect these words had upon him: 'Never did any passage of scripture come with more power to the heart of man than this did at this time to mine. It seemed to enter with great force into every feeling of my heart'.

After long meditation on the text, Joseph retired to the woods to ask God for enlightenment. What happened next forms the prelude to Joseph Smith's career as a prophet. No sooner had he knelt down and begun to pray than he was enveloped in darkness: despair overwhelmed him. Just as he was about to abandon himself to destruction, a light appeared overhead and descended upon him. Here is his own description of what followed: 'When the light rested upon me I saw two Personages, whose brightness and glory defy all description, standing above me in the air. One of them spake unto me calling me by name and said, pointing to the other — This is My Beloved Son. Hear Him!'

Joseph Smith was in no doubt that he was conversing with the divinity, and he quickly made known the purpose of his inquiry — to discover which of all the sects possessed the truth, which one he should join. In answer, he was told that he should join none of them, for they were all wrong: their creeds were an abomination and their priests were all corrupt.

The angel Moroni

Nothing else of any moment was revealed to Joseph Smith then, nor for the next three years. The visit of the Father and the Son was something he presumably kept to himself, for it was many years before the incident acquired any currency among Mormons. But on a night in September 1823, while preparing for bed, Joseph Smith had his second vision. An angel, who gave his name as Moroni, appeared and told him of a hidden book written upon gold plates containing an account of the ancient inhabitants of America, their religion, and their place of origin. The book, said the angel, represented the fullness of the Gospel as it had been delivered to these people by the Saviour. It was the divine will that Joseph Smith should be the instrument whereby God would effect a translation of the work. Deposited with the plates, and attached to a breastplate, were two seer stones known as the Urim and Thummim, which were to be used for the purpose of translation. So that he would know where the gold plates were hidden, Joseph was granted a vision in which the burial place was clearly revealed. The angel ended with a warning, however, that the time was not yet fulfilled when the plates should be obtained. Three times during that night the angel appeared to Joseph Smith and delivered the same message without variation.

These occurrences, which had occupied the whole of the night, had evidently taxed Joseph's strength. The following day he was unable to do his work, and on his way home from the fields fell into a swoon. He recovered to find the angel standing over him. Joseph was commanded to acquaint his father with the events of the previous night, then to go directly to the place where the gold plates were deposited. Joseph Smith found an eager listener in his father, for Smith Snr was a fervent believer in the importance of dreams and visions.[1] He told his son to do exactly as the angel had said.

Treasure from the earth
Guided by his vision of the previous night, Joseph Smith had no difficulty in locating the burial place, in the side of a hill just outside the village of Manchester. The plates, Smith relates, were contained in a strong-box, hidden under a large, partially-covered stone. He goes on: 'Having removed the earth, I obtained a lever, which I got fixed under the edge of the stone and, with a little exertion raised it up. I looked in, and there indeed did I behold the plates, the Urim and the Thummim, and the breastplate, as stated by the messenger.'

Joseph made to remove them but was prevented from doing so by the sudden reappearance of the angel Moroni, who indicated that the time for bringing them forth was not yet, but four years hence. Joseph meanwhile was to return to meet with Moroni on the same day every year, to receive further revelations and instructions, an obligation which he dutifully fulfilled.

In the meantime more secular affairs occupied Joseph Smith's time. He continued to work on the family farm, and was also actively engaged with others in work of a different nature, of which more will be said later.[2] On 18 January 1827 he married Emma Hale, daughter of Isaac Hale of Harmony, Susquehanna County, Pennsylvania, with whom Joseph had lodged about a year earlier. The marriage was not to Mr Hale's liking.

Finally, on 22 September, the four years of probation completed, the angel returned and delivered the gold plates into Joseph Smith's keeping. It seems that word about the existence of the plates soon got around: Joseph Smith complains of the attempts made by certain of his neighbours to get hold of them. Joseph and his wife were obliged to flee to the quiet of Emma's parents' home in Harmony, where the serious work of translation began.

Enter Martin Harris

In February of the following year Joseph and Emma received a visit from Martin Harris, a prosperous farmer who had befriended them earlier and assisted them with a gift of money. Harris had heard of the discovery of the gold plates and was very interested by this. By now, according to his own account, Joseph Smith had copied a considerable number of the characters from the plates and, with the aid of the seer stones, had managed to translate some of them. Harris was shown a paper containing some of the transcribed characters and the translations which Joseph had made. He asked if he might borrow the paper and, on receiving permission, set out with it for New York City.

Up to this point we have been following a narrative, for the veracity of which we have only Joseph Smith's word. Martin Harris's report of what took place in New York City is the first attempt to substantiate the story with anything that could pass for evidence. When Harris went to New York City he sought the opinion of the learned.

> I went to the City of New York, and presented the characters which had been translated, with the translation thereof, to Professor Charles Anthon, a gentleman celebrated for his literary attainments. Professor Anthon stated that the translation was correct, more so than any he had before seen translated from the Egyptian. I then showed him those which were not yet translated, and he said that they were Egyptian, Chaldaic, Assyriac, and Arabic; and he said they were true characters.

Harris alleged that Professor Anthon gave him a certificate certifying that the characters were genuine, but took it back and tore it up when Harris explained that the plates containing the text had been revealed by an angel. His report concludes: 'I left him and went to Dr Mitchell, who sanctioned what Professor Anthon had said respecting both the characters and the translation.'

Harris's account of this meeting with Professor Anthon appears in the personal history which Joseph Smith appended to the *Pearl of Great Price*. It is followed by a gap in the narrative. From other sources we know that Martin Harris returned to Harmony and became Joseph Smith's scribe, writing down what Smith supposedly was dictating from the plates, though Harris wasn't shown them. However, after two months of dictation, Mrs Harris, who disliked Smith intensely, got hold of the manuscript and refused to hand it back. It was never returned; it is reasonable to assume that Mrs Harris destroyed it. We can imagine Joseph Smith's dismay at this turn of events. According to the Mormon version, Smith consulted God on the advisability of beginning again, and God told him not to bother but to continue where he had left off. Consequently, the missing portion was never redone and, following this setback, Martin Harris's career as a scribe came to an end.

Enter Oliver Cowdery
About a year later, in early April, a young schoolteacher named Oliver Cowdery arrived at Joseph Smith's door. Cowdery had recently boarded with Joseph's family in New York State while pursuing his profession as a teacher. There he heard the account of the angel and the gold plates; fascinated by the tale, he decided to make Joseph's acquaintance. In Cowdery Joseph Smith found a ready convert, and the two men struck up an immediate friendship. Two days after his arrival in Harmony, when the work of translation recommenced, Cowdery became Joseph Smith's second scribe.

As the work proceeded, a strange tale unfolded. It appeared that the American Indians were the descendants of a party of Jewish immigrants, called after their leader Nephi, who had left Jerusalem towards the end of the seventh century BC. Most remarkably, the Nephites had once been Christians, for Christ had appeared among them shortly after his ascension and founded his Church there.[3] But this Church, like the one Christ founded in the Eastern hemisphere, eventually failed. The history, said to have been written in the language of 'reformed Egyptian', was the work of an ancient prophet named Mormon. It had been hidden in the ground by Mormon's son, Moroni, during a time of civil war. It was this same Moroni, now a resurrected being, who had appeared to Joseph Smith and entrusted him with the plates of the record.

While the translation was in progress, Joseph Smith was giving a lot of thought to the subject of baptism, as a result, he claimed, of encountering references in the Nephite record to baptism for the remission of sins. Since Joseph had never been baptised, he and Cowdery decided to question God concerning the matter. Accordingly, they went to the woods near the Susquehanna River and proceeded to pray. The story goes that while the two were engaged in prayer, they perceived a heavenly messenger who identified himself as John the Baptist, and explained that he had been sent by Peter, James and John to confer upon them the Priesthood of Aaron. In due time, he said, they would also receive the Priesthood of Melchizedek. Joseph Smith was to be known as the first Elder of the Church: Oliver Cowdery was to be the second Elder.

As instructed by John the Baptist, the two men went down to the river, and there Joseph Smith baptised Oliver Cowdery, after which Cowdery in turn baptised Joseph Smith. Then each ordained the other to the Aaronic Priesthood by the laying-on of hands. They returned home in joyous mood, but observing a self-imposed silence on the matter of their ordination to the priesthood and the appearance of John the Baptist — owing, as Joseph wrote, 'to a spirit of persecution which had already manifested itself in the neighbourhood'.

The three witnesses and the eight
During part of 1829, Joseph Smith and Cowdery stayed at the home of Smith's friend, David Whitmer, in southern New York State where, in June of that year, the translation from the gold plates was completed.

Evidently it occurred to Joseph Smith that his story would lack conviction unless he could come up with some sort of proof that the gold plates actually existed, and he set about obtaining sworn testimonies from several of his acquaintances. Initially, three people witnessed to the existence of the gold plates: Oliver Cowdery, David Whitmer and Martin Harris. Their testimony, the substance of which appears below, is to be found in the preface to the Book of Mormon.

> Be it known unto all nations, kindreds, tongues, and people, unto whom this work shall come: That we...have seen the plates which contain this record...And we also testify that we have seen the engravings which are upon the plates...And we declare with words of soberness, that an angel of God came down from heaven, and he brought and laid before our eyes, that we beheld and saw the plates, and the engravings thereon...

All three witnesses later left the Mormon Church, though none ever repudiated his testimony concerning the plates.

Shortly afterwards, Joseph Smith obtained testimony from a further eight witnesses. Their declaration also appears in the preface to the Book of Mormon.

> Be it known unto all nations, kindreds, tongues, and people, unto whom this work shall come: That Joseph Smith, Jun., the translator of the work, has shown unto us the plates of which hath been spoken, which have the appearance of gold; and as many of the leaves as the said Smith has translated we did handle with our hands; and we also saw the engravings thereon, all of which has the appearance of ancient work, and of curious workmanship. And this we bear record with the words of soberness, and that the said Smith has shown unto us, for we have seen and hefted, and know of a surety that the said Smith has got the plates of which we have spoken. And we give our names unto the world, to witness unto the world that which we have seen. And we lie not, God bearing witness of it.

Christian Whitmer	Hiram Page
Jacob Whitmer	Joseph Smith, Sen.
Peter Whitmer, Jun.	Hyrum Smith
John Whitmer	Samuel H. Smith

Here, the eight testify to having actually handled the plates. Of the eight, three subsequently left the Church, though it is claimed that none ever denied his testimony. After this evidence had been obtained, the angel Moroni reappeared, and the gold plates were handed over for ever.

The Church organised

Efforts were now made to have the manuscript published. Martin Harris mortgaged his farm to provide the necessary finance, and the 'Book of Mormon' left the press in the Spring of 1830.

Moves were also under way to bring about the re-establishment of Christ's Church, in accordance with directives to Joseph Smith from on high. The inauguration took place on 6 April 1830 in the home of Peter Whitmer of Fayette, Seneca County, New York. Present were members of the Smith and Whitmer families and Oliver Cowdery. It was to be known simply as the Church of Jesus Christ; the words 'Latter-day Saints' were added three years later. During the proceedings, Joseph Smith indicated that he had received a divine revelation appointing him a prophet and an apostle of Jesus Christ. The Aaronic and Melchizedek Priesthoods having already been instituted, other features were added within the next few years including the Quorum of the Twelve Apostles, and the office of the Seventy, derived from Luke 10:1-16.

Progress was promising; several of the leading members of the movement were converted during the first year, including Brigham Young. However, opposition grew and the Mormons, as they became known, had to leave New York and move west to Kirtland in Ohio where they established their own community.

They acquired property and founded a bank, which later failed. It was at Kirtland that the first Mormon Temple was built.

From Ohio a party of missionaries, which included Joseph Smith, left for Jackson County, Missouri. Here, according to a revelation Smith claimed to have received,[4] the Saints were instructed to build Zion, the new Jerusalem. For the next few years the Mormons were established in two settlements, in Ohio and Missouri, with their leaders in communication with each other. During this time Smith was continually receiving revelations. These were written down and incorporated in a volume of 'scriptures' known as *Doctrine and Covenants*. This, together with the *Pearl of Great Price*, the Book of Mormon and the Bible,[5] completes the quartet of works Mormons regard as scriptural.

Hostility continued to dog the Mormons' tracks, eventually driving them out of both settlements. Their beliefs and claims, involving an adverse judgement on all other faiths, antagonised their neighbours. Their practice of polygamy also scandalised many. Although the alleged revelation permitting the practice was made known in 1843,[6] Mormon leaders had entered into plural marriages long before then.[7] Also, some older settlers envied their prosperity, built up after hard, conscientious work. In the slave state of Missouri, the Mormons made themselves unpopular by opposing slavery. For these and other reasons the Mormons continued to suffer personal abuse and the destruction of their property. Joseph Smith himself suffered beatings, was tarred and feathered, and on more than one occasion was thrown in jail. Eventually, the Mormons took refuge in Illinois, where they built the city of Nauvoo, from where, in the summer of 1839, a party of Mormons left on the first mission to England.

Martyrdom

Illinois was but a brief sojourn for the Mormons, though it proved to be the end of the road for their prophet. Opposition to Joseph Smith had intensified, and not only from outsiders. Many of the faithful were disturbed by the new teachings that Smith was introducing into the Church; polygamy especially caused much disenchantment. In Nauvoo, several prominent Mormons left the Church and exposed Smith in the *Nauvoo Expositor*. He had the printing press and office of the *Expositor* destroyed and was charged with riotous behaviour. While Joseph and Hyrum Smith and two others awaited trial in Carthage, an ugly mood descended upon the town. On the evening of 27 June 1844, an armed mob stormed the jail. The Smiths died in a hail of bullets.

Smith's death led to an exodus of Mormons from Nauvoo. The largest group, under the leadership of Brigham Young, began the long trek westward to Utah. There the Brighamite Mormons founded a thriving community and city by the great Salt Lake.

2

The Mormon Story — A Critical Appraisal

However credible Mormons believe their case to be, it is unquestionably weakened by their inability to produce the gold plates. The testimony of the three and the eight notwithstanding, how immeasurably stronger their position would have been if only scholars had been allowed the opportunity of examining the plates! But since the heavenly messenger, Moroni, saw fit to withhold them from all but Joseph Smith and his intimate circle of acquaintances, it is to their testimony that we must turn, and to the expert testimony said to have been given by Professor Anthon.

Professor Anthon's statement
An early opponent of Mormonism, E.D. Howe, wrote to Professor Anthon in 1834 concerning Martin Harris's account of their meeting in New York City six years earlier. Professor Anthon replied at length, giving his own version of what occurred,[1] one which differed in some important respects from Harris's account. Professor Anthon complained: 'The whole story of my having pronounced the Mormonite inscription to be "reformed Egyptian hieroglyphics" is perfectly false ... the paper contained anything but Egyptian hieroglyphics'. Professor Anthon tells how his first inclination on examining the characters Harris showed him was to suspect a hoax. When Harris let it be known that he had been persuaded to sell his farm to obtain the money to publish the 'golden book', Professor Anthon changed his mind, suspecting a scheme to cheat Harris of his money. He told Harris of his suspicions. Anthon denied ever having given Harris a certificate testifying to the correctness of Joseph Smith's translation; indeed

he states quite plainly that he was never shown the translation of the characters that Smith claimed to have made.

A further anomaly concerns Dr Mitchell's part in the affair. Martin Harris stated that Dr Mitchell was the last person he called on, and that he was able to verify what Professor Anthon had said regarding both the characters and the translation. But according to Professor Anthon, it was to Dr Mitchell that Harris first took the paper, only approaching Professor Anthon on the recommendation of Dr Mitchell when the latter was unable to give an appraisal of the paper's contents.

The Mormon historian, B.H. Roberts, cites this letter in his own work,[2] and also another letter of Anthon's, written some seven years later and addressed to the Rev. Dr T.W. Coit, Rector of Trinity Church, Rochelle, New York. Roberts professes to find certain discrepancies in the two letters, which leads him to question Professor Anthon's reliability. Instead, he puts his faith in Martin Harris's account of their meeting.

But there are more puzzling aspects of this episode. The language of the gold plates was 'reformed Egyptian', a language which, according to the Book of Mormon itself, 'none other people knoweth'.[3] How, then, could Professor Anthon have verified Joseph Smith's translation had he seen it? And how does it advance the Mormon case to have Professor Anthon pronounce the characters on the paper 'Egyptian, Chaldaic, Assyriac and Arabic', when we are assured they were taken from an unknown language? It is plain that Martin Harris's journey to New York City could not have been anything but a futile venture; and the Mormon claim that Professor Anthon was able to pass judgement on the characters is highly suspicious, to say the least. What could well be the most revealing aspect of this affair is the fact that the Mormon version is based on Martin Harris's *verbal* report, eventually written down, not by Harris, but by Joseph Smith.

Are the witnesses dependable?
The testimony of the witnesses is pivotal to the Mormon case. But just how reliable is their evidence? We might also ask: why were those people chosen to bear witness and not others? Now, the claim to have unearthed a gold bible at the direction of an angel is something quite outside the ordinary course of events, and certain to provoke a sceptical reaction. If a disbelieving public was to be won over, the impartiality of those called to bear testimony would have to be beyond question. At the very least we should expect persons who had not had any previous connection with the business of the gold plates. Yet it is a striking fact that all eleven witnesses were involved in some way in the

production of the Book of Mormon. The subject of the gold plates was discussed freely in the Smith home for the four years of Joseph Smith's probation. Martin Harris and Oliver Cowdery had acted as scribes in the work of translation and the translation was completed in the Whitmer home. It is a most suspicious circumstance that the second group of witnesses was drawn exclusively from two families, the Smiths and the Whitmers.[4] It is not unreasonable to be reluctant to place any reliance on Joseph Smith's story of the gold plates when the only witnesses to their existence were members of Joseph Smith's own family and his closest friends.

Writing of the first group of witnesses, a Mormon author asks: 'Why should the world doubt? The testimony of three such men would convict any man in the courts of our land'.[5] Writing in the same vein regarding the eleven witnesses, another author informs us that 'all concerned were mature men of demonstrated judgment...'.[6] The facts do not support this verdict. Level-headedness was a trait foreign to every one of Joseph Smith's witnesses. Martin Harris was positively unstable. A firm believer in the everyday occurrence of the supernatural, Harris was in the habit of proclaiming prophecies and laying claim to divine revelations. Seeing a deer in the wood one day, and convinced it was Jesus in disguise, he accompanied it for two or three miles, conversing with it all the while.[7] On another occasion he spoke of an encounter with the devil who, he said, resembled a jackass. Fawn Brodie, Joseph Smith's biographer, tells us that Harris was met with 'amused tolerance and only occasional bitter scorn' from his fellow Mormons.

Oliver Cowdery was convinced of the truth of the story of the gold plates before ever he met Joseph Smith. Lucy Mack Smith, in her memoirs, observed that when Cowdery was living at the Smith home (at the time Joseph and his wife were living in Harmony, Pennsylvania) he was 'so completely absorbed in the subject of the record, that it seemed impossible for him to think or converse about anything else'.[8]

A Mormon historian[9] recalls Hiram Page, another witness, obtaining revelations with the use of a seer-stone. He was encouraged by Oliver Cowdery and the Whitmer family, all of whom believed in the power of Page's stone. Joseph Smith found out about it and immediately had a revelation manifesting the Lord's displeasure at these goings-on. Henceforth everyone save Joseph Smith was forbidden to have revelations. So the rival prophet's vocation was nipped in the bud.

Not so that of a young seer at Kirtland, Ohio who, in the summer of 1837, was attracting a considerable following from among the faithful. She claimed to receive revelations and to see the future in a black stone which she had in her possession. All three of Joseph Smith's first group of witnesses became her disciples, and their secret meetings were held in the home of David Whitmer, with whom the girl lodged.[10]

Upon such foundations rests Joseph Smith's 'Restored Church'. In such men Mormons would have us put our faith: to their testimony we are expected to give our unqualified assent. The alternative is surely hard to resist, even if there will always be a measure of uncertainty about precisely what took place. We have seen how, because of their close association with Joseph Smith, the eleven were predisposed to believe in the events they testified to. Assuming there was no conspiracy between Joseph Smith and the witnesses, it would appear that Smith deceived them in some way, either by trickery or by hypnosis. By every account we possess, Joseph Smith was a born leader who exercised a hypnotic power over people. Years later Oliver Cowdery was to write of Joseph's 'mysterious power, which even now I fail to fathom'.[11] Perhaps it had been this mysterious power which had convinced Cowdery that he had been visited by John the Baptist that day in the woods by the Susquehanna River. And perhaps it was this same power, possibly combined with trickery, that had persuaded the eleven that they had seen and handled the gold plates. Whatever the explanation, there is not the least doubt that the witnesses to whom Joseph Smith allegedly showed the gold plates, and from whom he managed to elicit testimony as to their existence, were lamentably lacking in credibility, being without exception credulous, superstitious, highly impressionable people. For this reason, if for no other, their testimony stands utterly discredited.

Is Joseph Smith dependable?
Once the Book of Mormon had been printed and circulated, and the new faith set on course, the enemies of the prophet were not slow in appearing. One of the first to take the offensive was an ex-Mormon named Philastus Hurlbut, who collected sworn statements impugning the character of Joseph Smith from over a hundred of Smith's former neighbours. The statements were later bought by E.D. Howe and appeared in his *Mormonism Unveiled,* an early and most devastating anti-Mormon book: they may be read in an appendix to Fawn Brodie's definitive biography of Joseph Smith.[12] These and other, similar statements are mentioned not because of any particular wish to denigrate the character of Joseph Smith, but because they shed light on his claim to be a prophet and, most especially, on his claim to have discovered a gold bible hidden in the earth.

The statements refer to Joseph Smith and his family having occupied their time digging in the earth for buried treasure. It was an occupation that Joseph Smith pursued both in New York and in Harmony, Pennsylvania. By virtue of a 'peak-stone' placed in his hat in such a way as to exclude all light, Joseph claimed to be able to locate hidden treasure. In this way, he was effective in directing not only members of his own family, but also other persons in the business of money-digging. It has been observed that in this early, money-digging phase of Joseph Smith's life, two characteristics emerged that were to play an important part in his subsequent career as a prophet: 'an ability to lead men older than himself, and a fertility of imagination'.[13]

Another critic who began inquiring into Joseph Smith's past was the Rev. John A. Clark, a contemporary of Smith's. Dr Clark researched the Smith family's neighbourhood to discover a history of money-digging. He too mentions the seer-stone and the hat which Joseph used to locate treasure.[14]

If we are to believe those who knew him, Joseph Smith's characteristic feature was his manner of speech, which has been described as 'exaggerated and extravagant'. This was the opinion of a number of his former neighbours and acquaintances, whose sworn statements appeared in an early history of Mormonism by Pomeroy Tucker.[15] No one, it was alleged, could ever rely on anything Joseph Smith said. This is consistent with the verdict obtained by Dr Edmund Fairfield, President of Michigan College, while visiting Palmyra, New York. All of Smith's acquaintances who volunteered an opinion concurred that Joseph Smith was 'simply a notorious liar'.[16]

This insight into Joseph Smith's character has obvious relevance in view of the claims he made: it was given some substance by a newspaper article written by Smith in a weak attempt to defend himself against the charges in Howe's *Mormonism Unveiled*. Smith felt constrained to admit to having had in his youth 'many vices and follies', and to having exhibited 'a foolish and trifling conversation'.[17]

The statements collected by Hurlbut and others should not be accepted entirely without reservation. Anti-Mormon feeling ran high in those early days; it also appears that people then had a peculiar fondness for signing affidavits. Nevertheless, it is impossible to dismiss them as merely the products of envious neighbours or sectarian hatred. The common emphasis on such features as the peak-stone and the hat have a ring of truth, and it is inconceivable that all should have conspired to invent a story of Joseph Smith having been a money-digger.

The Mormon response to these charges has been revealing in

its evasiveness. The charges have never been successfully challenged, Mormon writers contenting themselves, for the most part, with accusations of muck-raking. Joseph Fielding Smith, a descendant of the Prophet and the official Church historian, observes a total silence on the matter in his comprehensive work, *Essentials in Church History.*[18] Some writers have attempted to explain away Joseph Smith's money-digging operations, however. One such is Joseph Smith himself. In the historical sketch in the *Pearl of Great Price,* Smith relates an occasion when he was hired by a Mr Josiah Stoal to dig for a silver mine in the vicinity of Harmony, Pennsylvania. This, he states, was the basis for the money-digging stories. But he omits all reference to the peak-stone and the hat, and there is not a hint of the supernatural in his account. Describing the same episode, Lucy Mack Smith also neglects to mention the peak-stone and the hat, though she does refer to Mr Stoal's having chosen Joseph Smith to assist him in the digging of the silver mine 'on account of having heard that he possessed certain means by which he could discern things invisible to the natural eye'.[19] Though she avoids using the word, this is obviously a reference to Joseph's seer-stone. She also clearly implies that this was not the first occasion that Joseph Smith's powers had been put to use.

B.H. Roberts cites this incident as the origin of Joseph Smith's reputation as a money-digger and adds, significantly, that Joseph was hired to direct the digging because of his 'gift of seership'.[20] Elsewhere, Roberts expressly mentions the seer-stone, relating how Joseph found it while digging a well for a Mr Clark Chase of Palmyra, New York. Roberts adds: 'It possessed the qualities of Urim and Thummim'.[21]

Others who were not so coy about the precise manner in which the digging was directed have asserted that on the occasion that Joseph Smith worked for Mr Stoal he followed his usual procedure of using the peak-stone in the hat. His father-in-law, Isaac Hale, with whom Joseph lodged while in the employ of Josiah Stoal and before his marriage to Emma, was one of those who volunteered this information.[22] Moreover, despite the attempts by Smith's apologists to limit his money-digging activities to this one incident, it is certain that he was similarly employed in other parts of the locality.

The last word on the subject must go to Smith's biographer, Fawn Brodie, or rather to the documents she has unearthed.[23] The principal document is a court record, and concerns Joseph Smith's trial before a justice of the peace in Bainbridge, Chenango County, New York on 20 March 1826, at which Smith was charged with being 'a disorderly person and an imposter'. The document was first brought to light in the nineteenth century when it was published by Bishop Daniel S. Tuttle of Salt Lake City in his contributory article to an *Encyclopedia of Religion*. Five witnesses testified at the trial that Joseph Smith used a 'peep-stone' to locate buried treasure. On being questioned by counsel, Joseph Smith admitted to possessing a peep-stone, and to using it to locate lost property and buried treasure of various kinds in various places.

Fawn Brodie's biography of Joseph Smith was reviewed by Hugh Nibley in the Mormon journal, *Deseret News*; the review was later published as a pamphlet.[24] It made the charge that the court record in question never existed, but had been faked. Subsequent work by Mrs Brodie's associates, however, have authenticated the document thoroughly. One of her colleagues proved that Bishop Tuttle, who came by the record, had a female relative who was a court official at the trial of Joseph Smith. Further research resulted in the discovery of two independent newspaper accounts of the trial. Fawn Brodie and Bishop Tuttle had been vindicated. Later editions of her book contained this information. In the later (1974) edition of Nibley's pamphlet, all reference to the trial had been omitted.

Joseph Smith's proven money-digging activities must put a large question mark against his claim to be a divinely-appointed prophet. His claim to have unearthed a gold bible which he translated by means of the Urim and Thummim has obvious implications when viewed in the light of his early fascination for buried treasure and seer-stones. It is not without significance that an early criticism of Joseph Smith alleged that at first he claimed only to have discovered gold plates, and that the religious element in the story was a later addition.

Who wrote the Book of Mormon?
The authorship of the Book of Mormon has been the subject of much debate among those who do not accept its supernatural origin. There are two main theories: one holds that Joseph Smith wrote the work himself; the other that he wrote it in collaboration with someone else, possibly Sidney Rigdon. Moreover, some critics have held that in the writing of it, Joseph Smith, with or without a collaborator, plagiarised an earlier work, adapting it to his own purposes.

Those who favour the second theory believe it would account for the religious material in the book. Joseph Smith was largely uneducated, whereas Sidney Rigdon, a former Baptist minister, was a competent theologian, destined to have a formative influence on the development of the new religion. Mormons have always contended that Rigdon converted to Mormonism only after he had been shown the published Book of Mormon, and it must be said that the evidence that Rigdon ever knew Joseph Smith prior to then is only tenuous.

An alternative explanation for the religious content of the Book of Mormon is to be found in the psychological hypothesis known as 'dissociated personality'. Joseph Smith grew up against a background of intense religious ferment. All around him new creeds and ideologies clamoured for a hearing. It has been suggested that Smith may have absorbed, without fully understanding, the ideas he heard expounded and the biblical language in which they were expressed, and was able to 'recall and use them in his moments of visionary elevation'.[25]

One subject which possessed an irresistible hold on the imaginations of early nineteenth century Americans was the question of the origin of the American Indians. The explanation found in the Book of Mormon, that the Indians were descended from the Jews of the Old Testament, was not new, but it was the most widely-held theory of the day. There were many books on the subject then available which Joseph Smith could easily have read. One such book was Ethan Smith's *View of the Hebrews; or the Ten Tribes of Israel in America*. Ethan Smith's book was published in 1823, seven years before the publication of the Book of Mormon. Fawn Brodie, in comparing the two books, has made some interesting observations; it is worth quoting her at length.

> Both books opened with frequent references to the destruction of Jerusalem; both told of inspired prophets among the ancient Americans; both quoted copiously and almost exclusively from Isaiah; and both delineated the ancient Americans as a highly civilised people. Both held that it was the mission of the American nation in the last days to gather the remnants of the house of Israel and bring them to Christianity... *View of the Hebrews* made much of the legend that the 'stick of Joseph' and the 'stick of Ephraim' — symbolising the Jews and the lost tribes — would one day be united; and Joseph Smith's first advertising circulars blazoned the Book of Mormon as the 'stick of Joseph taken from the hand of Ephraim'.[26]

Ethan Smith's book also included a description of how copper breastplates with two white buckhorn buttons fastened to the outside of each plate had been discovered in Indian mounds, and told of how they resembled the Urim and Thummim of the ephod of the high priest of ancient Israel.

Was *View of the Hebrews* used as the basis for the Book of

Mormon? It does seem likely; as Fawn Brodie says, 'The striking parallelisms between the two books hardly leave a case for mere coincidence.' Or are we to believe that Ethan Smith miraculously acquired an extensive knowledge of the contents of the gold plates while they were still hidden in the earth, and before their existence had been disclosed to Joseph Smith? In the year that *View of the Hebrews* was published, and fully four years before he began dictating his translation of the gold plates to Martin Harris, Joseph Smith was holding members of his family enthralled with his detailed descriptions of the ancient Americans and their way of life.[27]

It would be highly satisfying to be able to resolve the question of the authorship of the Book of Mormon beyond all reasonable doubt; but it is of no great importance. For those who reject Joseph Smith's story, it is sufficient to show the book's human origin. Therefore the question which divides Mormons and their critics — Is the Book of Mormon of divine or human origin? — will be given greater attention in chapters 3-6.

PART II

The Book

3

Israelites in America

It might be thought that Mormons are unique in claiming to possess primary sources attesting to the origin of the American Indians. But others have produced 'ancient records', pretending to have translated them from secret tablets or indecipherable hieroglyphic texts.[1] Were it not for the religious content of the Book of Mormon and the circumstances connected with its origin, it might well have met with the obscurity surrounding those works which derive the Indians from lost Atlantis or Mu, of interest only to mystics and to students of human eccentricity. As it is, it becomes necessary, and is to the advantage of all concerned, that the claims made for the book be subjected to close scrutiny.

The chief events related in the Book of Mormon can now be summarised. The most ancient people written about were called Jaredites. Their ancestors are said to have left Mesopotamia at the time of the building of the Tower of Babel and, under divine direction, to have migrated to the western hemisphere, where they settled and multiplied. Mormons have credited these people with creating a great civilisation, comparable with any in Old World history. Jaredite civilisation lasted for almost 2,000 years before the Jaredites became extinct, a result of their interminable wars.

About 600 BC, at roughly the time the Jaredites disappeared from history, a group of Jews called Nephites were encouraged by their prophets to leave Jerusalem and make their way to America. They were joined some years later by a second wave of Jewish immigrants, the Mulekites. The two groups eventually merged and were thereafter known simply as Nephites. It is claimed for the Nephites that they attained great heights of civilisation.

The Nephites are described as a white and beautiful people. However, a number of them, having lapsed into wicked ways, were cursed by God with a dark skin, the curse being inherited by their descendants. The dark-skinned people and the whites who joined with them are given the name Lamanite. Nephites and Lamanites frequently warred with one another; until about 400 AD, when the Nephites met their end in a war of extermination. The passing of the Nephites brought to a close the Book of Mormon history, the victorious Lamanites subsequently degenerating into the wild state in which they were found by Europeans. All American Indians are held to be the descendants of the Lamanites.

Just before the Nephites met their end, the gold plates containing the abridgement of their sacred records were hidden in the earth by Moroni, to be brought forth in the latter days into the possession of Joseph Smith who had been chosen by God as the instrument of the restoration of his Church.

Despite the picture that has been presented of a succession of highly advanced civilisations, the Book of Mormon is very largely concerned with the conduct of war. Rebellion, mass destruction and the wholesale reduction of populations through warfare are recurring themes of the book. Nevertheless, it is possible to obtain some idea of the extent of material progress made by the people who figure in its pages.[2] Both Jaredites and Nephites possessed metals: tools, weapons and other instruments of war are detailed. Both peoples lived in cities and embarked upon programmes of urban building on a massive scale. Nephi, in a vision of his posterity granted him by an angel, is said to have beheld so many cities that he could not number them. These Nephite cities were connected by roads and highways stretching from land to land. Yet if the peoples of the Book of Mormon were great builders, they also destroyed much of what they built, and there is little in the book to indicate that what is being recorded is the history of a highly civilised people; quite the contrary.

The high point of the Book of Mormon is the account of Christ's appearance to the Nephites following his ascension, recorded in 3 Nephi 11-28. This is held to fulfil his statement found recorded in St John's Gospel: 'Other sheep I have, which are not of this fold: them also I must bring, and they shall be one fold, and one shepherd'.

After this visitation, Nephites and Lamanites alike joyfully embraced the Christian faith and there followed two centuries of untroubled orthodoxy. The third and fourth centuries, however, were marked by schism and gradual loss of faith, the Lamanites as a body apostasising shortly after 400 AD with the results described above. This falling away from the faith is described in the short book, 4 Nephi.

Mormons believe the genuineness of their sacred book to be abundantly supported by the evidence. They have shown great interest in the subject of Indian antiquities, and have been very active in studying the archaeological data of Middle America for the purpose of establishing that the creators of the pre-Columbian civilisations were none other than the Nephites of the Book of Mormon. Mormon missionaries have assured me that archaeologists are daily turning up new evidence to substantiate the Book of Mormon record. Mormons believe that the evidence clearly indicates that the ancestors of the Indians were Jews, and that Christ appeared to them in ancient times. The arguments set out below are those most frequently urged by Mormons in support of their beliefs. Although the last of the Nephites were driven north and met their end in New York State, where the plates were buried, Mormon writers, including Joseph Smith, have designated Middle America the land of the Book of Mormon.[3] Therefore, the following account refers chiefly to those early civilisations of Mexico and the adjacent area which emerged during the centuries accounted for in the Book of Mormon.

The Indians as Jews
There are four 'facts' adduced as proof that the Indians were once Jews.

1.   It is alleged that archaeology and ethnology reveal the Indians to be Jews. Archaeological sites throughout Middle America reveal architectural remains — statues, stelae, door lintels and temple carvings — depicting bearded men with aquiline features, some wearing long robes. Typical of these finds is a stele discovered at the Olmec site of La Venta, on the coastal region of the Gulf of Mexico. The carving, nicknamed 'Uncle Sam' by archaeologists, represents a bearded, hook-nosed man. According to Milton Hunter, the Mormons' foremost authority on archaeological matters, it 'strongly resembles a Jewish priest of pre-Christian times'.[4]

Smaller artefacts bear similar testimony: vases, pottery, figurines, clay heads and mirrors, all decorated with images of hebraic-like men, have been unearthed in Maya and Olmec sites in Mexico, while sites in Peru have yielded pottery of like decoration. Mormons contend that the frequent appearance of semitic-looking figures on pre-Columbian artefacts corroborates the explanation of Indian origins given in the Book of Mormon. Dr Hunter reminds us that the Hebrews and the Nephites of the Book of Mormon were bearded, whereas the Indians have very little facial hair.

About half of Milton Hunter's book, *Archaeology and the Book of Mormon* is devoted to the author's efforts to establish the existence of tribes of white-skinned Indians. To accomplish his task, Hunter travelled extensively in Middle America, visiting villages and museums, studying murals and reading Indian and early Spanish writers. It will be recalled that the Lamanites were cursed with a dark skin for rebelling against their more righteous brethren, the Nephites. In the final battle which led to the extermination of the Nephite race at the hands of the Lamanites some Nephites changed sides. Dr Hunter's research has led him to the conclusion that the white Indians of Middle America are descended from those apostate Nephites.

2. Certain features of Old Testament life are duplicated in New World cultures. Circumcision, arranged marriages, food taboos, markets as foci of trade and social life, brick-making and salt-manufacture are suggested as common traits. Milton Hunter cites the Spanish Carmelite, Antonio Vazquez, himself a believer in the Hebrew origin of the Indians, who observed that Indian priests underwent a form of anointing, wore their hair long like the Nazarites, and offered animal and child sacrifices. Perhaps the most extensive treatment of the subject is to be found in Thomas Stuart Ferguson's *One Fold and One Shepherd*. Here the author has compiled an alphabetical list of close to 300 cultural traits common to Bible lands and Middle America in ancient times. The presence of Old World cultural traits in pre-Columbian America leads Mormons to assume an historical connection, lending support to their belief that ancient America was colonised by Jews from Asia.

3. The linguistic evidence, say Mormons, shows Indian languages to be radically Hebrew. In an article entitled 'The Language of the Book of Mormon',[5] Elder George Reynolds writes of the conviction of several of the early Spanish writers that some of the Indians spoke a corrupt Hebrew. He alleges the discovery of native tombstones bearing Hebrew inscriptions, and relates how travellers in North and South America heard the natives exclaiming the sacred words, Yehovah and Halleluyah.

Milton Hunter and Thomas Stuart Ferguson in *Ancient America and the Book of Mormon* note that the Maya word for dowry is identical to the Hebrew word for the same custom. In *Why I Believe*, a work of Mormon apologetics, George Edward Clark includes a short word-list which he claims shows a striking similarity in terms of phonetics and in comparable meanings between native Mexican and Hebrew. This, he says, substantiates the Book of Mormon claim that the Nephites were Hebrews who migrated from Jerusalem.

4. Mormon writers have expended much time and energy proving that Old Testament beliefs were known to the Indians and were recorded by their scribes. Early travellers in the New World frequently remarked upon the Indians' apparent knowledge of events related in the Bible. Some of the Spanish missionary priests made the same observation. Bishop Bartolomé de Las Casas, for example, who wrote a history of the Indians, writing of the Maya Indians of Guatemala, refers to their traditions of the flood, the end of the world and final judgement of fire.[6]

A more telling statement of Indian belief would appear to be that preserved in the annals of Indian scribes. The Quiché Maya book, *Title of the Lords of Totonicapán*, claims a Hebrew origin for the Maya, mentioning Abraham and Jacob by name, and relates how their ancestors came from the east when a passage opened in the sea.[7]

The *Popol Vuh* of the Maya of Guatemala also contains an account of a miraculous parting of the sea, and tells of a flood, a high tower and a confusion of tongues. The Maya god, Tohil, is represented as handing down sacred law to a priest on a mountain top.[8] Legends concerning a flood, a high tower and a changing of languages are to be found in the Mexican book, *Annals of Ixtlilxochitl*, which is cited by Hunter and Ferguson in their own book, *Ancient America and the Book of Mormon*. Mormons see the explanation for the occurrence of these traditions in their having been passed on by the Indians' Hebrew ancestors.

Christ in America
We come now to the evidence purporting to show that Christ visited America in ancient times. Clark, in *Why I Believe*, has remarked how, when the Spaniards arrived in the New World, they found among the Aztecs symbols of the cross, a fact which to Clark is explicable only on the supposition that Christ had visited the Aztec's ancestors, as is claimed in the *Book of Mormon*. A common tradition in the Americas told of a great cult hero who had come among the people and given them their religion and their laws. The Mexican name for this person is Quetzalcoatl, a

word meaning feathered serpent. Ixtlilxochitl says that Quetzalcoatl was considered 'just, saintly and good', adding that he taught by example.

Mormons believe that Quetzalcoatl and Christ are the same person. The many feathered serpent motifs which have appeared in archaeological sites they hail as symbolic representations of Christ. Just how the symbol of the feathered serpent came to be attached to Christ is explained by Milton Hunter.

> As the quetzal bird flew through the air and the brilliant rays of sunlight reflected the resplendent gorgeousness of the colours of its plumage… it may have reminded the ancient Americans of the beauty and glory of Jesus Christ who had descended from heaven through the air to visit them and later had returned into heaven in like manner… what could be more appropriate to the minds of those people in symbolising the central character in the greatest event that had occurred in the New World than to take as a symbol for him the beautiful quetzal bird?[9]

Allied to the symbol of the quetzal bird is that of the serpent which, says Hunter, from the earliest times represented the crucified Christ, his healing and life-giving powers.[10] It was following the close of Book of Mormon history, according to Hunter, that the reprobate Lamanites changed Christ's name to Quetzalcoatl. Hunter quotes the explorer and writer, Von Humboldt, on the Mexican belief that Quetzalcoatl was 'both God and man', and cites Prescott on the widespread belief in his second coming. Lord Kingsborough, a nineteenth century collector of Indian antiquities, is cited for his observations that Quetzalcoatl is portrayed in Indian art as a person crucified.

4

Are the Arguments Convincing?

It may already have become apparent that Mormon writers are not always consistent when arguing their case. Milton Hunter can differentiate bearded 'Hebrews' and beardless Indians, forgetful of the Mormon belief that the latter are descended from the former. This fundamental error recurs throughout Hunter's writing. On page 32 of his *Archaeology and the Book of Mormon* is stated the plainest of contradictions. Writing of Maya motifs he asserts firmly that 'These bearded men are definitely not of Indian type but are of Hebraic type', yet five lines on we come across the statement: 'The ancestors of the American Indians...were Hebrews'.

Dr Hunter's penchant for having it both ways is further in evidence when, having contrasted bearded images with smooth-faced Indians to infer a separate Jewish strain, he endeavours, by reference to the white skins of these same Indians, to decide their Jewish ancestry also.

The incongruity of describing an eastern Mediterranean people and their immediate progeny as 'white and exceeding fair'[1] might be overlooked, but it must be asked why those Nephites who had deserted to the side of the Lamanites were not cursed with a dark skin as the Lamanites before them had been. And why were their descendants spared this ignominy when we read in 2 Nephi 5:23 that the seed of apostates must bear the curse? The presence of white Indians would tend to undermine the claim that the Book of Mormon is a true and reliable record. If the book is to be trusted, there should be no white Indians at all.

Further, the arguments purporting to prove from archaeology that the Indians are descended from bearded semites, if allowed, would serve equally well certain other theories of Indian origins. Assyrians, Canaanites, Tyrian Phoenicians, Carthaginians and the remnants of the Lost Tribes of Israel, all of whom having at one time or another been suggested as the ancestors of the Indians, would appear to have an equal claim on the evidence.

The Indians are not one physical type

The truth is that the evidence points overwhelmingly to the conclusion that the American Indians do not constitute one physical type, but are an extremely mixed race. Early sculptures of Middle America reveal not only the semitic-looking figures already referred to, but also those of a broad-nosed type with distinctive thick lips and slanted eyes.[2] Ruth Underhill of the United States Indian Service had made some pertinent observations regarding the diversity of Indians. 'We now know', she writes, 'that Indian complexions vary from dark brown to yellow and even white...their hair might be brown or black...their noses anywhere from the Roman type, seen on the Indian penny, to a small snub nose or even a flat one.'[3] Alvin Josephy Jr who, like Ruth Underhill, is a US government expert on Indian affairs, devotes a chapter of his book, *The Indian Heritage of America*, to the diversities of Indians. After detailing specific physical differences, he continues: 'In general, from one end of the hemisphere to the other, Indians exhibit many physical variations; there is not the slightest resemblance between a New York Iroquois and a Brazilian Cayapo, between a Montana Crow and a Mexican Maya'.[4] Such complexity in physical make-up would seem to be a clear refutation of the facile arguments of Mormon writers purporting to prove a Jewish ancestry for the Indians.

The anthropologist's approach to trait distribution

Robert Wauchope, who is director of the Middle American Research Institute and Professor of Anthropology at Tulane University, has drawn attention to the fact that at the time of the Spanish Conquest the Old Testament was virtually the sole documentary source for the study of primitive cultures; the ancient Hebrew ethnology, consequently, was the only primitive way of life known in any great detail. It seems not to have occurred to early writers that similar customs and usages can develop independently of one another. When customs known to be associated with Bible lands began appearing in the New World the tendency was to assume a historical connection. Mormons, disregarding a century of progress in anthropological science, make the same mistake. But the same line of reasoning has linked wandering Israelites with the Afghans, Japanese,

Burmese, Malays, various African tribes, and even the Anglo-Saxons.[5] Professor Wauchope puts the whole matter in perspective in a way which sums up the anthropological approach to the question of trait distribution. 'Today you can go to the Human Relations Area Files at any one of many universities, ask for an inventory of all the peoples of the world who practice some particular custom...and in a relatively short time you can have all the known examples, together with the detailed data and history of each'.[6]

The fact that certain Old World cultural traits have a New World counterpart is much less revealing than the adverse fact that certain others do not. Among Old World traits not to be found in America at the time of its discovery were proverbs, oaths, ordeals, divination by examination of viscera, the plough, the potter's wheel,[7] stringed musical instruments (except the monotone bow), stock breeding, and the use of milk and of dung fertiliser,[8] and Mormons must explain how these elements came to be lost following the arrival in the Western Hemisphere of Nephite culture bearers.

Indian languages and linguistic games
The practice of matching words of different languages in order to prove an historical connection is not a Mormon invention; most theories of Indian origins have been bolstered by linguistic evidence. Early this century Professor Leo Wiener of Harvard assembled some 3,000 Maya-Mexican and African words in an attempt to demonstrate his thesis that the Maya and Nahuatl languages are derived from Mandingo.[9] Robert Wauchope tells how he himself produced a list of some fifty near-duplications between English and Maya in order to 'dent the armour' of a Hungarian student of his who, in his own lengthy word-list, had matched Finno-Ugrian and Yucatec Maya words, convinced that the two languages were historically related.

The practice has a long history. An early debunker of such linguistic juggling was Edward John Payne of University College in America who, in 1899, brought out long word-lists showing striking similarities between Mexican Nahuatl and Greek on the one hand, and between Mexican Nahuatl and Latin on the other. Unlike the Mormons and others intent on proving their pet theories, Payne was concerned to demonstrate the fact that coincidences, even in unrelated languages, are simply unavoidable. Given the inclination, it is not too difficult to prove that the Indians spoke English, or Greek, or African Mandingo, or probably any language that the Mormons care to name.

Mormons appear to have no conception of what the study of

41

comparative linguistics involves, and naively suppose that it is simply a case of matching words of similar sound and meaning. But the problem of Indian languages is very complex. Indian language experts speak in terms of dialects, language groups, parent stocks and superstocks; and there is general agreement on one thing — that there was never a time when all Indians of the American continent spoke the same language. Ruth Underhill thinks it likely that the early migrants brought their languages with them; these then flowered into a multiplicity of dialects as the people dispersed.

Precisely how many languages were spoken in the Americas will never be known, for many of them have become extinct. At the time the Europeans arrived more than 2,000 were in use;[10] over 300 were spoken in Mexico and Central America.[11] Some linguistic experts have arranged the Indian languages of the United States into six enormous families each, as Ruth Underhill remarks, 'as different from the others as English from Chinese'.[12]

All this suggests a great antiquity for Indian languages. The Mayan scholar, Michael Coe, has observed that Mayan languages, though closely related, are yet 'mutually unintelligible...the result of a long period of internal divergence'.[13] He puts the point in time at which this divergence is thought to have commenced at about the middle of the third millennium BC, 2,000 years before the advent of Hebrew-speaking Nephites.

But the difficulties facing Mormons do not end there. The work of linguists is further complicated by the numerous phonetic differences. These have been described by Josephy. 'In many of the Indian languages certain consonants are whispered or are not pronounced. In some, the sounds of k,p, or t are uttered with constricted throat muscles, as if the speaker were being choked. Some Indian tongues possess tonal characteristics like those of the Chinese; changes in the pitch of a vowel, for instance, completely alter the meaning of a word or an expression'.[14] It will be appreciated by now that, other arguments considered, the enormity of the language problem alone militates against such an uncomplicated view of Indian origins as that held by Mormons.

Presence of Old Testament beliefs — an alternative explanation
What on the face of it might seem a more formidable body of evidence tending to the support of Mormon claims is the written testimony of European and native Indian historians pertaining to Indian beliefs.

But is the evidence really so formidable? The early missionary priests, it must be emphasised, were not trained anthropologists.

Not all of them, indeed, can escape the charge of incredulity. We can well imagine the misunderstandings arising from language difficulties, added to the confusion caused by the missionary zeal of the fathers and the natives' eagerness to please. Missioners' reports concerning Judaeo-Christian beliefs among the Indians, at a time when anthropology as a science did not exist, must therefore be regarded with a degree of caution.

Also, it is a matter of some consequence that the Maya books, the *Popol Vuh* and the *Totonicapán*, were not written down until the middle of the sixteenth century, and the Mexican *Annals of Ixtlilxochitl* were not written down until about 1600: all three, therefore, post-date the Spanish Conquest by many years. Scholars attribute the similarities in the contents of these books and the contents of the Bible to European influence on the Indian scribes, who doubtless had been exposed to Christian teaching by the time they committed their own traditions to writing. Ixtlilxochitl, whose *Annals* are much quoted by Mormon writers, was employed by the Spaniards as an interpreter and received Christian baptism. In addition, the frequently propounded theory that Christian missionaries reached the New World before Columbus, is entertained as a possibility by scholars and should not therefore be overlooked.

The real Quetzalcoatl
Mormons face stiff competition in their efforts to prove an identity for Quetzalcoatl. An enigmatic figure of Indian folklore, Quetzalcoatl has at various times been identified as Atlas, St Thomas the Apostle, Votan, Osiris, Poseidon, Dionysus, Bacchus, a Buddhist or Brahmin missionary, Viracocha and Mango Capac of Peru and Hotu Matua, the cult hero of Easter Island.[15] To this multifarious company Mormons would have us add the person of Jesus Christ.

It can be stated as a fact that the feathered serpent motif did not evolve in the way that the Mormon writer, Milton Hunter, says it did. A carving of a figure in jaguar head-dress accompanied by a feathered serpent has been unearthed at the Olmec site of La Venta[16] which has been established by archaeologists to have flourished from 800 to 400 BC.[17] Thus the symbol is much older than Mormons imagine and pre-dates by many centuries the event they say it represents. A quite different explanation of the origin of the feathered serpent motif is to be found in the article on Quetzalcoatl in the *Encyclopedia Americana*. Here we are informed that in the earliest Indian beliefs the quetzal bird was a cloud symbol and the snake a symbol of the whirling wind. The two eventually became attached to the god, Quetzalcoatl, who

43

was regarded as the chief wind god and 'the presiding deity of the air'.

The presence of the cross in pre-Columbian America is also explained. Symbolic crosses are, of course, universally present in human history and are older than Christianity itself. Here the cross was another symbol of Quetzalcoatl in his capacity as chief wind god, being a representation of the four regions of the earth, from which came the four winds. Though crucifixion was widely used anciently as a means of execution, there is no evidence to suggest that it was ever practised in the New World. The 'crucifixion' noted by Lord Kingsborough is the Morning Star sacrifice, a Mexican ritual in which the victim was bound to a scaffold and then pierced by an arrow.[18]

There are, nevertheless, good reasons for believing that the legend of Quetzalcoatl the cult hero owes more to history than it does to subsequent embellishment, though it has nothing to do with the appearance of Christ in America, nor of any of the other people suggested. Archaeology and tradition combine to furnish the details. Quetzalcoatl was one of many gods worshipped throughout Mexico in ancient times. When the Toltec capital of Tula was founded, shortly after the middle of the tenth century, the founder-ruler, Topiltzin, introduced the worship of the feathered serpent, Quetzalcoatl, *and took his name.*[19] From this event, it seems, originates the confusion of deity and cult hero, which gave rise to the incarnate god of Indian folklore written of by Von Humboldt.

Some years later the devotees of a rival god achieved power and Topiltzin Quetzalcoatl and his followers were banished from Tula. According to legend, before he left Topiltzin promised to return one day — doubtless the origin of the second coming referred to by Prescott. The legend was preserved down to Aztec times, for Moctezuma thought he saw the promise fulfilled in the arrival of Cortés and the conquistadores.

Topiltzin Quetzalcoatl, after some wandering, came to the Gulf Coast and took to the sea. Due east across the Gulf of Mexico lies the Yucatan peninsula, homeland of the Yucatan Maya. Maya traditions record the arrival from the west of a great personage named Kukulcan (the Maya word for feathered serpent) at some time in the second half of the tenth century, when a people known as the Itza also appeared in Yucatan. About the same time a series of new buildings appeared at the great Maya centre of Chichen Itza in Yucatan displaying sculptures identical in many details with those at Tula.[20] Dr Bushnell of Cambridge writes: 'The coincidence is too great for there to be any serious doubt that Kukulcan and the Itza were the Toltec Quetzalcoatl and his followers who had been expelled from Tula not long before'.[21] Thus the various strands in the Quetzalcoatl legend find their explanation in the career of the Toltec ruler, Topiltzin, who can be firmly placed in history as living more than nine centuries after the time Mormons say Christ preached to the Nephites.

5

Archaeology and the Book of Mormon

Ever since their discovery by Europeans the problem of the origin of the American Indians has fascinated us. Probably no other subject has so stimulated the imagination, or provided such a classic illustration of what Glyn Daniel has termed 'the tendency in mankind to seek for the comforts of unreason'.[1] The ingenuity of Indian origins theorists has known few bounds.[2] Almost every Old World people has at some time or another been proposed as the ancestors of the Indians. On less solid ground, historically and geographically, but no less self-assured, have been those enthusiasts who have suggested lost continents, either Atlantis in the Atlantic or Mu in the Pacific, as the Indians' place of origin. Still others, whose originality at least commands admiration, have reversed the direction of the migrations, arguing that the genesis of human life took place in America, and that what we call the Old World is actually the New. A variant theory, but one containing ideas from these last two, has civilisation originating in Atlantis, from whence it was exported to America and from there to Egypt.[3]

It is important, then, that we see the Mormon thesis in its proper context, as being one among many professing to explain the origin of the American Indians. The vagaries of inspired amateurs apart, what light can the sciences of anthropology and archaeology shed on the subject?

The true origin of the American Indians
It is now generally accepted by anthropologists that the New World was first peopled by migrants of Mongoloid extraction who crossed the Bering Strait from Asia to Alaska in separate waves

many thousands of years before the birth of Christ. Most scholars suggest the period of between 15,000 and 30,000 years ago, though some think America may have been peopled at a much earlier date, perhaps as early as 100,000 BC. There could have been no migrations later than 8,000 BC, for by that time the landbridge which provided the entry route would have been submerged beneath the sea.[4] Mormons put the date for the first occupation of America, when the Jaredites arrived from Mesopotamia, at about 2,200 BC.[5]

Skeletal evidence and a continuous trail of functionally linked archaeological artefacts over northern Europe, Asia and much of North America attest to the origin and progress of these first Americans, while a considerable body of evidence bears witness to the early date of the occupation.

The earliest finds to be dated with certainty are of about 10,000 BC and are associated with the invention of a type of stone point knows as Clovis. Clovis points have been found throughout North and Middle America with the remains of the mammoth and the horse.[6] There is evidence to show that while the hunting of these beasts was taking place, people were living in caves in Illinois, Alabama and Missouri.[7] A cave in Nevada has revealed sloth bone tools, wooden darts and the remains of a camp fire extinguished about 8,500 BC.[8] Sandals discovered in a cave in Oregon were worn over 9,000 years ago.[9]

South America, which was populated from the north, has also yielded notable finds in the form of stone tools discovered in the region of the desert coast of Peru and dated about 8,500 BC.[10] Michael Coe has reported on radio-carbon dating which has shown that men were hunting sloth, horse and quanaco, a member of the camel family, at the Straits of Magellan by at least 9,000 BC.[11] Dr Coe is of the opinion that most of South America may have been populated long before then.

As yet, not all scholars are agreed as to the exactness of some of these early dates but, as Glyn Daniel observes, 'what there is no disagreement about is that man, that is to say the earliest American Indian, was in what is now the United States of America by between 12,000 and 10,000 BC.'[12] If we take the most conservative date, then, there is still a considerable gap of some 8,000 years between the time anthropologists say the Americas were peopled and the time Mormons say the Jaredites arrived from the Tower of Babel.

Mormons have been forced to concede the body of evidence favouring the Mongoloid theory of Indian origins. Hunter and Ferguson make an important admission in their book, *Ancient America and the Book of Mormon*. 'It is clear,' they write, 'that some

47

of the ancestry of some of those people entered the New World from northeastern Asia by way of Bering Strait. They left a trail of primitive artefacts behind them.'[13] Aware no doubt of the embarrassing degree to which their own account of the first peopling of America differs from that widely held by Americanists, Mormons have been at pains to circumvent the obvious conclusion. Hunter and Ferguson, for example, remind us that the Book of Mormon nowhere claims to account for all people who entered the New World in ancient times. This attempted wriggling out of an awkward situation represents a shift in position on the part of Mormon apologists and even contradicts the word of their own prophet, Joseph Smith, who was most emphatic that the New World was occupied by only two groups of people anciently, the Jaredites and the Israelites.[14] Elsewhere, Milton Hunter has sought to reconcile Mormon dogma and scientific fact. 'Following the close of Nephite history,' he writes, 'many Mongolians came to America and mixed with the Indians.'[15] But note the inference that it was the Book of Mormon people who arrived first. Note also the clear affirmation that the Mongolian migration followed 'the close of Nephite history'. Since Mormons assign to the former event the extremely late date of 600 BC, and to the latter event the even later date of 400 AD, the scientific evidence is still very much against them, whatever concessions they feel they are making to the Bering Strait theory.

The myth of imported cultures

According to the Mormon writer, Milton Hunter, each group of people mentioned in the Book of Mormon brought the culture of its own country to the Western Hemisphere: 'and so the beginnings of human life in the New World were represented by cultures fully developed and not by savage, primitive nomadic hunters'.[16] But this is a flat contradiction of the position taken by every authority in the field of American pre-history. Some Trans-Pacific contact from south-east Asia at a late date is deemed not unlikely by scholars, but the notion of an imported full-blown culture is rejected as a fanciful myth. The American civilisations, argues Gordon Willey, stand 'clearly apart and essentially independent from the comparable culture core of the Old World'.[17] Stuart Piggott makes the same point on page 8 of the general editor's Preface to Bushnell's *The First Americans*. He maintains that the independent direction taken by Old and New World cultures had already begun by the tenth millennium BC. Glyn Daniel enumerates three points on which he says scholars are in general agreement: the first peopling of America, the independent American origin of agriculture, and the synoecism in Nuclear, that is Middle, America. Each of these points when enlarged upon can be seen to be at variance with the notion of imported cultures, and each is fatal to the acceptance of the Book of Mormon as a genuine record of the history of ancient America.

The archaeology of Middle America

New world archaeology is distinguished by the absence of many features usually associated with civilised life. The following are some of the more striking examples.

1.   Contrary to what the Book of Mormon states, and to what Mormons claim archaeology reveals, the natives of the New World hardly ever lived in cities. True cities 'were rare anywhere in the aboriginal New World, especially in Mexico'.[18] The word is sometimes used indiscriminately to describe the ceremonial centre which was the focus of religious and social life in Middle America but which Bushnell considers was more akin to a cathedral close. Some of the ceremonial centres of the immediate pre-colonial period had urban populations, but they were by no means usual. In any case they do not concern us, as they fall well outside the period spanned by the Book of Mormon.

There is only one exception during the centuries accounted for in the Book of Mormon: the ceremonial centre of Teotihuacán, which flourished in the Valley of Mexico from about 100 BC to 600 AD, can rightly be described as a city, in that it was surrounded by the dwellings of the people. Elsewhere the people lived in scattered villages, travelling to the ceremonial centres to attend the temple ritual or to shop at the markets, which were a regular feature of Middle American life. Of the many cities which proliferate among the pages of the Book of Mormon, and of those whose destruction is so graphically recorded therein, no trace has as yet come to light.

2.   New World archaeology reveals a complete absence of metals. When the Spaniards arrived in the New World they came upon civilisations that had only just emerged from the Stone Age. The Incas of Peru possessed a few bronze tools made from metal obtained in streams, and a few copper tools were in use in parts of Mexico, but metallurgy as a craft was of a relatively recent date. The great buildings of Middle America and Peru were constructed entirely with stone tools.[19] Metals were unknown in Mexico before 900 AD.[20] Josephy maintains that the art of metallurgy was introduced into Middle America from the south in Toltec times,[21] that is about the tenth century AD.

What, then, are we to make of the iron age civilisations described in such detail in the Book of Mormon? So far as is indicated by the present state of archaeological knowledge, there is not the slightest evidence that any civilisations so described ever existed. No iron, steel or brass, no chariots, swords, shields, breastplates or any form of armour have ever been recovered from pre-Columbian archaeological sites.[22] The metal objects frequently mentioned by Mormons — the gold ornaments and copper chisels dredged from the sacred Maya well at Chichen Itza, for example — post-date the close of Book of Mormon history by many centuries.

3. The Indians could not have had any use for the many roads and highways mentioned in the Book of Mormon, for they had no wheeled vehicles,[23] though the discovery of wheeled toys is proof that at least the principle was known. Transportation was limited to the canoe and, in the case of land transport, to litters borne by men. The reason why the wheel was never put to practical use is to be found in the absence of domesticated animals suitable for draught purposes. The ox, the horse and the ass which the Nephites, and the Jaredites before them, are said to have possessed were introduced into America by Europeans, as were the cattle, sheep and swine which the Jaredites are supposed to have domesticated.[24] The only domestic animal known to both hemispheres was the dog. Elephants, said to have inhabited the land in the days of the Jaredites, have departed without trace: not one skeleton has been found in any archaeological site.

Mormons make much of the fact that the bones of horses have been found in archaeological sites together with human artefacts and are correct when they argue that this indicates the contemporaneous existence of the horse and the early American. However, in Mormon thinking, the early American was no earlier than 2,200 BC. The native, pre-historic horse was hunted to extinction during the Ice Age.[25]

4. No civilisation can develop without some effective means of food production. The emergence of high civilisations in pre-Columbian America was made possible by the cultivation of maize, beans and squash. Early remains of these crops have been found in dry caves throughout the Americas. These are quite different crops from those of the Old World. The 'wheat and barley' and 'all manner of grain' mentioned in the Book of Mormon were nowhere present in the New World scheme of food production.[26] The absence of all the Old World fruit trees[27] is also curious, considering that the Jaredites are said to have

brought with them 'seeds of every kind', and the Nephites are also supposed to have had the foresight to take seeds with them when they departed from Jerusalem. The absence of the plough has already been noted. Indian farmers employed the slash and burn method to clear the ground, and tilled the soil by means of the digging stick. New World agriculture, in short, had none of the crops and none of the cultivation techniques of the Old World.

The pre-Columbian civilisations, then, uniquely lacking many of those features common to civilised life in the Old World, which features are given prominence in the pages of the Book of Mormon, have proved an unsuspected trap for the author of that work.

The religion of Middle America

The Book of Mormon tells how Nephite prophets from the earliest times provided knowledge of the Christian gospel in advance, so preparing the way for the coming of Christ. It further relates how for three centuries after Christ's appearance in ancient America the Nephites possessed a full Christian civilisation. Surely, then, we can expect to find a superabundance of Christian iconography among the archaeological remains? Such is not the case, however, though the architecture of Middle America is dominated by religion.[28] But which religion?

From the earliest times agriculture and ritual were closely associated: religion was bound up with the fertility of the crops.[29] Maize, the staple crop of the New World, was even made a god. This association continued through the high civilisations: Christopher Dawson finds the explanation for the amazing achievements of the Maya in astronomy in the development of the ritual cycle based on the agricultural year.[30]

The earliest Middle American civilisation was that of the Olmecs of the Gulf Coast. Olmec religion centred upon the belief in a race of were-jaguars, infantile monsters who were believed to be the result of the union of a jaguar and a woman. These creatures are everywhere present in Olmec sites. In function they were heavenly rain spirits, according to Bushnell 'the forebears of all the rain gods of Mesoamerica'.[31]

Michael Coe has traced the metamorphoses of these rain gods and finds the Iazpan culture on the Pacific coast near the Guatemalan border of crucial importance as a connecting link in time and space between the Olmec culture and that of the Classic Maya.[32] The Iazpan Long-Lipped God, a development of the Olmec were-jaguar god of rain, is transformed into the Maya rain god, Chac, or Long-Nosed God. A continuity of belief regarding the principal nature god is thus maintained.

The decipherment of many Maya glyphs has revealed a society dominated by religion, in which art, architecture and learning all served religious ends. As well as the rain god, the early religion of the Maya included the god of maize, a god of wind, and the fire god, Itzamna. Added to these in Classic times, beginning (in Mormon chronology) about a century before the close of Book of Mormon history, were the bacabs, who were four in number and supported the sky at each corner, a death god, gods of the upper world, the under world and the calendar, as well as many others.[33]

By about 300 AD all Mexican peoples shared a pantheon of gods, the main ones being the Rain God, his consort, the Water Goddess, the Sun God, the Moon Goddess, and the Feathered Serpent, who required the sacrifice of butterflies and snakes.[34] Archaeology bears powerful witness not only to the strength of these religious beliefs, but also to their great antiquity.[35] It should be remembered that it was throughout this period, according to Mormon belief, that Middle America witnessed first the florescence then the gradual decline of the Christian Church.

If, as Mormons contend, Christ visited America after his resurrection, then the most likely site of the cradle of Christianity there would be Teotihucán, near present-day Mexico City. Teotihucán was a great city centre whose influence radiated throughout Mexican and Mayan centres. At its height it covered an area of more than eight square miles: its estimated population was about 60,000.[36] Michael Coe thinks it was comparable with the Aztec Empire, perhaps bigger. Josephy stresses the third century as the period of its greatest brilliance and influence. Teotihucán, then, was a flourishing metropolis during that marvellous age of peace and righteousness which, according to the Book of Mormon, had been inaugurated by Christ.

Nothing remotely connected with the Christian gospel has ever been uncovered at Teotihucán, though many gods of the Mexican pantheon are represented there.[37] The temple pyramid of Quetzalcoatl, built about 250-300 AD and partly covered by a later structure, bears sculptures of the feathered serpent god,[38] alternating with rain god masks. The rain god is also depicted in wall paintings.[39] Teotihucán, then, exhibits much the same iconography as has been observed everywhere in Middle America. In the age of Origen and Cyprian in the Old World, the most primitive paganism was the religion of the New.

Who were the Nephites?

Who, then, were the peoples who appear on the pages of the Book of Mormon? How do they fit within the compass of pre-historic America? They are said to have brought forth great civilisations. The summit of achievement in pre-Columbian civilisation was that attained by the Maya, who are often called the Greeks of the New World. They excelled at mathematics and astronomy and their calendar was more accurate than the Gregorian Calendar which we use. Maya architectural remains are scattered throughout parts of Mexico, Guatemala and Honduras. Are the Maya the Nephites of the Book of Mormon?

Nephite history, we are told, lasted from 600 BC to 400 AD. The Maya were building temples and ceremonial centres towards the end of this phase; but the golden age of Maya civilisation, when the arts and sciences reached their apogee, was the Classic period of 300-900 AD.[40] Yet this was the age when the degenerate Lamanites are said to have ruled the land, beginning with the wars which led to the extermination of their Nephite brethren. Hunter and Ferguson in *Ancient America and the Book of Mormon* give the year 322 AD as the beginning of Lamanite dominance. They further assert that the substitution of Lamanite domination for the more refined Nephite influence would be reflected in the archaeological discoveries made in the area. In other words, the rule of the barbaric Lamanites would have resulted in an artistic and cultural eclipse. That is as we should expect. But Maya civilisation reached a high point at precisely that time when, in Mormon chronology, the Nephite nation was in decline, and continued to flourish throughout the post-Book of Mormon period of Lamanite decadence.

From the Book of Mormon, moreover, we learn that the Nephites were city-dwellers: yet it is said of the Maya particularly that they were a civilisation without cities.[41] Dr Bushnell draws our attention to the impossibility of building cities in the forests where the great Maya centres were located, and adds that elsewhere the work was prevented by the topography.[42]

A further difficulty arises when we consider the frightful wars waged by Book of Mormon peoples, for whom genocide seems to have been a way of life. Although the Maya are believed, on the evidence of wall paintings, to have made occasional raids on other people, possibly to obtain sacrificial victims, they were on the whole a peaceful people. Their ceremonial centres had no fortifications, and were for the most part located in places incapable of defence.[43] Maya art, Bushnell informs us, exhibited a high degree of continuity, based as it was on 'a stable culture which was undisturbed by wars against people of similar status'.[44] And Michael Coe has contrasted the 'untroubled serenity and sophistication' of the art styles of the Classic stage with the 'tough and fearful productions of later times'.[45] The age of strife and unrest among the Maya is associated with post-Classic times and the beginning of a general militaristic era which saw the warlike Toltecs and Chicimecs established in Central Mexico.

Since, as we are assured, the Nephites brought with them to the New World their own fully-developed culture, it is at the very least reasonable to expect that some remnants of this culture will have yielded to archaeological investigation. We think of those basic things necessary for the start of a new life in a strange environment — tools, weapons, lamps, pottery, for example — and the more personal and everyday things that any migrants might be expected to take with them, such as combs, jewellery, belt buckles and sandals. We think also of how articles of a practical and/or sentimental value tend to be handed on in families from generation to generation. Yet, amazingly, not a single object manufactured in the Old World has been found in any Maya site.[46]

We have thus far considered the Maya in isolation, as representing the highest point of pre-Columbian civilisation. But the Maya, unlike the Nephites of the Book of Mormon, benefited from outside influence. It has been established beyond all doubt that the Maya and all other Middle American civilisations rest ultimately on an Olmec base.[47]

The people who are given the name Olmec have been credited with possessing the earliest culture of Middle America, one with a distinctive art style and religion. Olmec pottery, sculptures and objects of art have been found far and wide:[48] Teotihuacán, and the centre which succeeded it in Mexico, Monte Alban, are both said to show Olmec influence, as are other centres, including the Maya. Olmec remains have been dated as belonging to a period as early as 1,200 BC,[49] and since the Nephites did not reach America until 600 BC, their designation as this 'mother culture' is clearly not possible. And if Olmec culture was the dominant influence behind all later civilisations, as Michael Coe and others believe, and was itself in full bloom when the Nephites arrived in the land, just where does the imported Nephite culture fit in? The question is of vital concern to Mormons: we leave it to them to suggest an answer.

The Olmecs, then, represented the parent culture of Middle America, if not of the whole continent, and neither they nor the Maya who followed and surpassed them can in any way be identified with the Nephites of the Book of Mormon. This raises one final question: could the Olmecs have been Jaredites, the first people accounted for in the Book of Mormon? The answer has to be in the negative, and for reasons very like those which have consigned the Nephites to the realm of fiction. The Jaredites had an urban civilisation: the Olmecs never lived in cities. Much the greater part of Jaredite civilisation, as described in the book of Ether, is co-terminous with the hunting and early agricultural stage of development in ancient America. Sedentary communities, when they finally became established, were organised around small hamlets of no more than a few families, and this was the arrangement when the Olmecs were building their ceremonial centres. It is estimated that the ceremonial centre of La Venta could have supported a population of no more than 150 people, comprising the ruling class and their attendants, and that these were supported by about 18,000 peasants living in villages scattered over a wide area of the countryside.[50]

Moreover, the Jaredites of the Book of Mormon were warlike, even genocidal. Though there are signs of violence at the Olmec site of La Venta, in the form of defacement of statues, nevertheless the disorder is believed to be associated with the abandonment of that site.[51] The almost endless state of war which prevailed among the Jaredites is not reflected in the archaeology of the Olmecs, whose peaceful arts were diffused over a wide area of Middle America.

Furthermore, the peak of Olmec civilisation was reached at precisely that stage when the Jaredites, exhausted by years of continual warfare, were on the point of extinction. We have it on no less an authority than Joseph Smith himself that the Jaredites were destroyed about the time of the Nephite immigration,[52] that is, about 600 BC. Talmage, on page 284 of his *Articles of Faith*, gives the date of the extinction of the Jaredites as 'near 590 BC.' Radio-carbon dating at the principal Olmec site of La Venta spans the centuries from 800 to 400 BC:[53] after the abandonment of La Venta Olmec culture survived in other areas for several centuries.[54]

Notwithstanding all these considerations, it is the common verdict of scholars, as we have seen, that human progress in the Americas, from the first primitive hunters to the creators of the high civilisations, manifested a continuity of development that was quite independent of Old World stimulus. The conclusion is surely inescapable. Serious, one might say insurmountable, difficulties face anyone attempting to accommodate the people written about in the Book of Mormon within the context of what is known of pre-Columbian civilisations.

6

The Internal Evidence

The writing style

In their efforts to vindicate their sacred book, Mormon authors have made much of what they see as its internal consistency. They profess to find a marked diversity of literary style throughout the book, particularly noticeable, it is said, when earlier prophets such as Nephi are compared with the later prophets, Mormon and Moroni.[1] They have attempted an analysis of the book's vocabulary: Clark claims to find 578 words that are exclusively Nephi's, and 683 words used by Alma and no other writer.[2]

Clark also notes the absence of modern words, listing over forty words descriptive of things pertaining to Joseph Smith's day, but not found in the Book of Mormon. This is held as further evidence that Joseph Smith translated rather than wrote the book.

This last argument is less impressive than it seems, for only an artless bungler would attempt to pass off as the ancient record of a vanished tribe a work containing words such as shot-gun, pistol, rifle, cannon, newspaper, pope, cardinal, and the names of modern religious denominations. These are a sample from the aforementioned list of words, whose absence from the Book of Mormon Clark seems to find so significant.

The claim made for diversity of writing style is difficult to sustain. Most of the verses in the Book of Mormon begin with the word 'And'. Common verse beginnings occurring in every constituent book of the Book of Mormon are: But, Wherefore, Now I, And now I, And now my brethren, And now my beloved brethren, And it came to pass, behold, Now behold, And now behold, For behold and But behold.

Considering the limited vocabulary of the book, the Nephite

prophets had an uncommon preference for certain words and phrases. The word 'continual' or 'continually' is common to every writing prophet except the author of 4 Nephi, a work of only forty-nine verses. The word 'speedy' or 'speedily' is much favoured by the first prophet, Nephi, as well as the last prophet, Moroni; also by Jacob, Enos, Mosiah, Helaman and the author of 3 Nephi.

The Nephites always 'labour diligently' and 'search diligently'. The word 'diligence' and all its variants appears frequently in the books of Nephi and Moroni, and in those of many of the intervening prophets also. But the word used to a monotonous degree by every Book of Mormon prophet is 'exceeding' and 'exceedingly'. In Jarom, a work of only fifteen verses, it occurs five times. It is to be found in such secondary works as the Record of Zeniff, which is preserved in Mosiah, and in the Epistle to Lachoneus, which is quoted in 3 Nephi 3, as well as in the main body of these books; and recurs with great frequency in the ancient Jaredite record, the Book of Ether.

The distinctive phrase 'after the manner of' or, alternatively, 'after this manner' is used by every writer except Helaman and the author of the short work, 4 Nephi, though Helaman has 'in this manner'. An unusual word used to describe civil and religious unrest is 'contentions', which is often contained in a phrase, the more usual being 'wars and contentions'. This phrase occurs in Jacob, Enos, Jarom, Omni, Mosiah, Alma, Helaman, 3 Nephi and Ether. Variations are: 'contentions and destructions' (1 Nephi, Enos), 'contentions and dissentions' (Mormon, 3 Nephi, Jarom), 'contentions and disputations' (4 Nephi), 'serious contentions' (Omni, Helaman) and 'much contention and many dissentions' (Helaman). The only Book of Mormon prophet to avoid using the word entirely is Moroni, in a work of only twelve pages.

What is indicated, then, is not diversity, but uniformity of writing style, such as one would expect in a work written entirely by one person. But, to turn from the writing style to the content of the book, Joseph Smith fell down rather badly here too.

Patriarchs, kings and prophets

To anyone only moderately acquainted with the Bible the Book of Mormon holds endless surprises. It is not simply that whole chapters of the Bible appear on its pages. Mormons have a plausible explanation for this: when they left Jerusalem in 600 BC the Nephites took with them copies of such of the Hebrew Scriptures as had been committed to writing at that time. Still, whether studying the book in earnest or merely browsing among its pages, it is impossible to avoid the growing conviction that the author plagiarised the Bible. There are several reasons for thinking this.

In following the vicissitudes of the Book of Mormon peoples as they become established on the American continent, the reader is repeatedly reminded of near-identical incidents narrated in the Bible. This is more in evidence in the Book of Ether, where frequent and blatant incidents of 'borrowing' should convince all but the most credulous. A small book of about thirty pages, placed towards the end of the Book of Mormon, Ether tells of the Jaredites, the first occupants of America. The narrative, dull and repetitive for the most part, assumes a certain fascination when read in the light of Old Testament history.

In the early chapters the relationship of Jared and his brother recalls that of Abraham and Lot, and the promises made by God to Jared's brother are exactly the same as those made to Abraham. The covenant with 'the true and only God' is established. Curiously, it is not Jared who is the principal protagonist in this history, but the unnamed brother, in whom is combined something of the personality and stature of Abraham, Moses and Samuel. After many years wandering in the wilderness, he receives a revelation on a mountain top and is commanded to write down what he has seen (Ether 3). Jared's brother, having led his people for many years, eventually grows old. The people then ask that a king be anointed to rule over them, a request fiercely resisted by their leader, but to no avail.

At first the Jaredites prosper under the monarchy. However, the second king, Kib, has to deal with the rebellion of his son, Corihor (ch. 7), an event which recalls Absalom's rebellion against David. Corihor's younger brother, Shule, a man noted for his wisdom (vv. 8 and 11), sides with his father, before succeeding him as king. During his reign the kingdom is divided: for a time there are two kingdoms, like Israel and Judah in the Old Testament. Later, God raises up prophets who condemn the wickedness and idolatry of the times. Their warnings go unheeded, however, and some, like Jeremiah, are cast into pits and left to die (ch. 9).

Most intriguing perhaps, is the account of Riplakish, a king who has many wives and concubines, taxes the people sorely, builds a beautiful throne and many spacious buildings, and reigns for forty-two years before his people rebel against his rule (ch. 10). King Solomon, who is clearly the inspiration for Riplakish, as for Shule, reigned for forty years.[3]

Whether Mormons puzzle over this unusual catalogue of parallel incidents we know not. We find it astonishing that within the compass of the first ten chapters of the book of Ether, there can be found what amounts to a potted history woven from a succession of key events in the historical books of the Old Testament.

Elsewhere, examples of this sort are scattered, but are not unremarkable. Thus in chapter 27 of Mosiah the conversion of Alma parallels that of St Paul, except that Alma is struck dumb. The story of Salome is recalled in Ether 8, wherein the daughter of Jared arouses Akish by dancing before him, then demands the head of the good King Omer as the price of her hand in marriage.

In Alma 10:2, Aminadi, like Daniel, is said to have interpreted writing made upon a wall by the finger of God. Here the writing is made on the wall of a temple; in the Bible account it appeared on the wall of Belshazzar's palace.

Certain descriptive passages in the Book of Mormon narrative echo the words of the Bible with uncanny accuracy.[4] In the account of Alma's conversion the angel of God is heard to exclaim: 'Alma, arise and stand forth, for why persecutest thou the Church of God?' 1 Nephi 18 describes the calming of a storm at sea, concluding in verse 21 and with the words 'and after I had prayed the winds did cease, and there was great calm'. All of which makes it extremely difficult to believe that the author hasn't dipped into the Bible for inspiration.

The King James Bible
The Book of Mormon, it has been said, contains lengthy extracts from the Hebrew Scriptures: it also includes a great deal of New Testament material. This is partly explained by the preaching mission Christ is supposed to have made to the Nephites; although, that Christ should have used exactly the same words on separate occasions, and had his sermons arranged in exactly the same way by independent scribes might strike the more thoughtful reader as too much of a coincidence. The Sermon on the Mount is reproduced word for word in 3 Nephi: 12-14.

Then, from the earliest times the Nephite prophets, unlike their Hebrew counterparts, were granted a clear vision of the future as it affected Jesus Christ, his death and resurrection. This vision extended to a knowledge of the central truths of the Christian faith. The difficulties involved in presenting a Christian theology centuries before the birth of Christ were overcome by having the Nephite scribes employ the simple device of adding 'which is to come' whenever an insight into the Christian message is given, and 'who is to come' whenever reference is made to the person of Christ.[5] So amazingly clear is the Nephite understanding of Christianity, at times it anticipates the very words used by the gospel writers centuries later.[6]

The inclusion in the Book of Mormon of large blocks of Old and New Testament material has proved a source of embarrassment to Mormons, as it has raised critical difficulties of which Joseph Smith can have had little or no conception. Not the least of these difficulties is the fact that the Bible extracts are word for word transcriptions from the *King James Bible,* which was published in 1611 and which could not therefore have been known to the Nephite prophets. Mormons reply to this objection by pointing out that Joseph Smith, in translating, would naturally write in the idiom of his own time and place, and this idiom was the language of the *King James Bible,* the translation widely used in Joseph Smith's day. But this is to miss the point entirely, for the criticism does not refer to *idiomatic expression,* but to *exact verbal reproduction.* The distinction, which should be apparent, will become clearer still if, for illustration, we compare the same text as it appears in two modern translations of the New Testament: the *New English Bible* and *Today's English Version,* though the same results would be obtained by comparing any two modern language versions. The text is taken from the Sermon on the Mount.

Look at the birds of the air; they do not sow and reap and store in barns, yet your heavenly Father feeds them. You are worth more than the birds! Is there a man of you who by anxious thought can add a foot to his height? And why be anxious about clothes? Consider how the lilies grow in the fields; they do not work, they do not spin; and yet, I tell you, even Solomon in all his splendour was not attired like one of these. (Mt 6:26-30; *New English Bible)*	Look at the birds flying around: they do not plant seeds, gather a harvest, and put it in barns; your Father in heaven takes care of them! Aren't you worth much more than birds? Which one of you can live a few more years by worrying about it? And why worry about clothes? Look how the wild flowers grow: they do not work or make clothes for themselves. But I tell you that not even Solomon, as rich as he was, had clothes as beautiful as one of these flowers. (Mt 6:26-30; *Today's English Version)*

Both versions are in the language of the present day. Yet, while both preserve the essential meaning of the passage, the choice of word and phrase differs to a marked degree. Here is the same passage as it appears in the *King James Bible* and in the Book of Mormon:

Behold the fowls of the air: for they sow not, neither do they reap, nor gather into barns; yet your heavenly Father feedeth them. Are ye not much better than they? Which of you by taking thought can add one cubit unto his stature? And why take ye thought for raiment? Consider the lilies of the field, how they grow; they toil not, neither do they spin: And yet I say unto you, that even Solomon in all his glory was not arrayed like one of these. (Mt 6:26-30; *Authorised King James Version,* 1611)	Behold the fowls of the air, for they sow not, neither do they reap nor gather into barns; yet your heavenly Father feedeth them. Are ye not much better than they? Which of you by taking thought can add one cubit unto his stature? And why take ye thought for raiment? Consider the lilies of the field how they grow; they toil not, neither do they spin; And yet I say unto you, that even Solomon in all his glory, was not arrayed like one of these. (3 Nephi 13:26-30; *Book of Mormon*)

Here it is not the case of different, though idiomatically similar, translations, as in the first example, but of supposedly different translations that nonetheless show *identical wording and turn of phrase.* Can there be any real doubt that the author of the Book of Mormon copied from the *King James Bible,* and therefore was not some fifth century Indian scribe, but someone who lived after the publication of that bible?

More errors
Having recourse to the *King James Bible* was Joseph Smith's undoing in more ways than one, for it resulted in the repetition of errors occurring in that version which more recent translations have been careful to avoid. Modern translations of the Bible, including all revisions of the *Authorised King James Bible* from 1881 onwards, omit the doxology at the end of the Lord's Prayer — For thine is the kingdom, and the power, and the glory, for ever — as it is believed to lack authenticity. Joseph Smith did not know this, hence the full version of the Lord's Prayer, including the doxology, is present in the Book of Mormon, as it is in the unrevised *King James Bible.* Other errors which occur in the King James Bible and are duplicated in the Book of Mormon are documented by the Baptist writer, W.R. Martin, in his highly informative book, *The Maze of Mormonism.*

Joseph Smith committed another *faux pas* when he included Isaiah 48-51 and 53 in the Book of Mormon. The Nephite prophets could not have possessed these texts. It is now a widely-held view of scripture scholars that Isaiah was the work of at least three authors, and that the eighth century Isaiah was responsible for chapters 1-39 only.[7] Chapters 40-55, known as Second or Deutero-Isaiah, was the work of an unknown prophet living in Babylon towards the end of the Exile. Since the Exile lasted from 587 to 538 BC, and the Nephites left Jerusalem in 600 BC, they could not have taken with them any part of the Book of Isaiah beyond chapter 39, as the rest of the book had not yet been written.

While certain aberrations in the Book of Mormon have come to light as a result of a better understanding of the Bible, others simply defy common sense. One wonders how it was possible for a Book of Mormon scribe to have been so familiar with the teaching of St Paul to include in his own work passages from 1 Corinthians 12-13.[8] And how could the prophet, Ether, have told the ancient Jaredites of the New Jerusalem to be erected in the land of America, when he and they knew nothing of the Old Jerusalem? Also, one marvels at how an institution such as the synagogue could have emerged independently as a fact of Jewish life in both the Old World and the New.[9] Synagogues were unknown at the time the Nephites left Jerusalem. These are but a few examples; many more could be cited.

Corrections to the Book of Mormon

Equally devastating has been the criticism which imputes the integrity of the Mormon bible. Mormons frequently maintain that the Book of Mormon has come down to us unchanged since the first edition of 1830. This is untrue. It is possible to compare recent editions of the book with the original, for it and other early Mormon literature are preserved in the Berrian Collection in the New York City Public Library. W.R. Martin researched these documents to find more than 2,000 changes in the Book of Mormon over a period of 131 years;[10] changes resulting not only from the correction of mis-spellings and awkward grammar, but from words and phrases being omitted from or added to the text.

Some changes are more serious than others. King Mosiah of Mosiah 21:28 underwent a change of name, God evidently suffering a lapse in concentration when, in the original edition of the Book of Mormon, the king's name was given as Benjamin.[11] Martin has shown that Mormon editors have even on occasion altered the doctrinal content of the book in places where it relates to the person of Christ.[12]

Yet Mormons are most insistent that the translation of their Book of Mormon was effected, not through human, but through divine power. The esteemed Mormon writer, James E. Talmage, is perfectly clear about what this means: 'It is noticeable that we make no reservation respecting the Book of Mormon on the ground of incorrect translation. To do so would be to ignore attested facts as to the bringing forth of that book.'[13]

Talmage's unequivocal statement is consistent with the accounts of how the gold plates came to be translated. Martin Harris was Joseph Smith's first scribe. His version was preserved by an early writer.

> By the aid of the Seer Stone, sentences would appear and were read by the Prophet and written by Martin, and when finished he would say 'written'; and if correctly written, the sentence would disappear and another appear in its place; but if not written correctly it remained until corrected, so that the translation was just as it was engraven on the plates, precisely in the language then used.[14]

David Whitmer, who was not a scribe but, nevertheless, a close friend of the Smith family and one of those who penned a testimony to the existence of the gold plates, has left us this version.

> A piece of something resembling parchment would appear, and on that appeared the writing. One character at a time would appear, and under it was the interpretation in English. Brother Joseph would read off the English to Oliver Cowdery, who was the principle [sic], and when it was written down and repeated to Brother Joseph to see if it was correct, then it would disappear, and another character with the interpretation would appear. Thus the Book of Mormon was translated by the gift and power of God, and not by any power of man.[15]

Though differing in some minor details, the two versions are substantially in accord. Both exclude the possibility of error, even the smallest grammatical error, in the manner in which the Book of Mormon was translated. In presuming to correct their bible, Mormon editors have thus represented God as an absent-minded semi-literate whose revelation, even regarding his own Son, they have not scrupled to treat as suspect and subject to revision.

It is probably too optimistic to expect these chapters to produce a dramatic change in attitude, should any Mormons read them.

Whenever the unreasonableness of their position is pointed out to them, Mormons invariably fall back on their standard reply — they invoke the authority of Joseph Smith as the last word on the subject. In the final analysis the informed judgements of scholars, the mass of accumulated evidence, common sense even, all count for nothing against the word of God's prophet. For Mormons, Joseph Smith settles all arguments. Mormons are entitled to their beliefs, but we in turn can expect them to be consistent. We are invited to consider the evidence. Having done so, we find that, so far from the evidence confirming the credibility of the Book of Mormon, as Mormons contend, it impugns it at every point.

PART III

The Cult

7

A Restored Church?

It is claimed for Mormonism that it is a restored Church. Mormons say that Christ founded a Church when he was on earth, but that it failed almost before it got off the ground. This is what Mormons call the Great Apostasy. This apostasy, begun in apostolic times, continued unabated down the centuries. With the calling of Joseph Smith, however, Christ's Church was re-established in its fullness, with all the offices and practices Mormons believe existed in the beginning.

It is clear that Mormonism stands or falls on this conviction that the Christian Church failed. For if it can be shown otherwise, then a restoration of the Church is neither necessary nor possible, and Mormonism would then be completely refuted. Mormons readily agree, confident in the belief that the evidence of Scripture and history supports their conviction.

How Mormons misuse scripture

Mormons believe that the apostasy of the Christian Church was foretold in sacred scripture. James E. Talmage explains: 'The foreknowledge of God made plain to Him even from the beginning this falling away from the truth; and, through inspiration, the prophets of old uttered solemn warnings of the approaching dangers.'[1] Talmage quotes Isaiah 24:5 and Jeremiah 2:13 as proof texts. According to LeGrand Richards certain of the Old Testament prophecies can only be appreciated in the light of the knowledge of the universal apostasy of the Christian Church. He instances Amos 8:11-12, and Micah 3:5-7.[2]

Now it is well known that Bible texts, when used by the unlearned, can be made to prove almost anything. This is especially true of apocalyptic texts, which deal with visions, and which are expressed in symbolic language. Mormons make no distinction between these and other texts, but treat all Bible texts alike. Apocalyptic language is difficult to understand and might be expected to pose problems for Mormons, who pride themselves on their lack of proficiency in scriptural exegesis.[3] This does not prevent them from quoting freely from such apocalyptic texts as the Book of Daniel, the Book of Revelation and Isaiah 24.

Also, it is important that Bible texts should not be taken out of context. To understand what the prophets are saying it is necessary to set their teaching against the background of the times in which they lived. An appreciation of the social, political and religious conditions which influenced their message is an essential requirement. A favourite text used by Mormons to prove the prediction of the apostasy of the Christian Church is Amos 8:11.

> Behold, the days are coming, says
> the Lord God,
> when I will send a famine on the
> land;
> not a famine of bread, nor a thirst for
> water,
> but of hearing the words of the
> Lord.

Amos was a shepherd from Tekoa in the southern kingdom of Judah who, shocked by what he saw in Israel in the north was moved to prophesy. Society in Israel was corrupt. Lip-service was paid to religion while everywhere the poor were oppressed. Looming on the horizon was the giant shadow of Assyria, whose armies were soon to invade and bring to an end the kingdom of Israel. Here we are presented with a familiar theme: a falling-away of Israel from friendship with Yahweh, God, followed by the call to repentance, and God's punishment of his unrepentant people, seen in the military defeats inflicted upon Israel. Isaiah and Micah must also be read in this context. Over a century later Jeremiah had to contend with the religious effects on Judah of Manaseh's apostasy, and the threat to that kingdom from the latest power to achieve ascendancy in the Fertile Crescent, Babylon. This is how we begin to understand these texts. It is to their own people and their own times that the prophets address themselves. That is not to say that they have nothing to say to us. But their chief concern is Israel's relationship with Yahweh; and when they complain of backsliding they refer not to a Christian, predominantly gentile, Church of the future, but to Israel's estrangement from Yahweh. To suppose that the Old Testament prophets are addressing themselves over the centuries to the religious conditions of the Christian era is misguided; and to quarry selected texts from the prophets in support of such a view, as Mormons do, is a patent misuse of Scripture.

The same method is used, and the same criticisms of the method apply, when Mormons profess to find in sacred Scripture predictions of the restoration of the Church through Joseph Smith. LeGrand Richards, taking as his text Revelation 14:6,7, comments: 'John saw the bringing back of the gospel to the earth to be preached to every nation, kindred, tongue and people.'[4] Several texts of St Paul are pressed into service as additional proof.

The Book of Revelation was written to bring strength and comfort to the Christians of John's day, who were undergoing persecution. The symbolism is not easy to understand, but what is perfectly plain, both from the opening verses of the book and from the concluding chapter, is that the author believed that the end of the world was at hand, and that the events he described would soon take place. This belief in the imminence of the end of the world was common in the early Church. We know this from St Paul's letters to the Thessalonians and his first letter to the Corinthians. Moreover, it seems clear from 1 Corinthians 7:25-32 that St Paul himself shared this view. It is, therefore, difficult to see how John and Paul could have been pre-announcing the advent of Joseph Smith's restored Church, expected eighteen centuries hence, when both believed that the end of the world would come in their time.

How Mormons re-write history
What form did this apostasy take? It seems that almost from the first the Church to which Christ had promised his enduring presence[5] lost its way: on the death of the Apostles it was left 'drifting...without any general authorities'.[6] Members of the Church soon became 'embroiled in endless controversies among themselves'.[7] The simple precepts of the gospel were forgotten and, in the absence of any central authority, true religion was everywhere corrupted by the introduction of heretical beliefs. According to Mormons, this was the condition of the Church in the second century.

The teachings of the Gnostics, Talmage tells us, were 'among the early and most pernicious adulterations of Christian doctrine'. For emphasis Talmage dipped into Eusebius and found a passage by Hegesippus outlining the heresies prevalent in his day and naming their proponents.[8]

Now this spectacle conjured up by Mormons, of a body in hopeless disarray, fits very well the theory requiring a restoration: alas, it does not fit the facts. Their first mistake is in failing to understand the nature of Gnosticism and its relationship to Christianity. Gnosticism was not something central to the Church, but a movement older than Christianity itself which sought a synthesis of all religious truths. When efforts were made to incorporate the new religion within the system, the Church stubbornly resisted.

Mormons are also wrong when they imagine that the truths of Christianity are so simple as to preclude further discussion of them. St Mark tells us that Christ had to give special explanations of his teaching to the Apostles, when the multitude was left to work it out for themselves.[9] The first great Christian commentator was St Paul, whose epistles developing the truths of the Faith are accepted by Mormons. St Paul, moreover, is not always easy to understand, as St Peter remarks in one of his epistles.[10] Early in the life of the Church, people naturally sought to clarify the sort of questions that were occupying their minds: what was the precise relationship of the persons of the Trinity? In what sense was Christ both God and man? There is abundant evidence to show that although legitimate discussion of the truths of the Faith was taking place, a clear distinction existed between the orthodox religion of Jesus Christ, faithfully preserved and transmitted by the Church, and the beliefs of those early religious innovators who had departed from the truth. To confuse the two is to commit a fundamental error.

Eusebius contrasts the transient nature of the heresies with the permanent, unchanging teaching of the Church: '...one after another new heresies were invented, the earlier ones constantly passing away and disappearing into different ways at different times into forms of every shape and character. But the splendour of the Catholic and only true Church, always remaining the same and unchanged, grew steadily in greatness and strength...'[11]

Far from embracing heresy, the Church imposed penalties on its proponents. Irenaeus informs us that the heretic, Cerdo, while living in Rome, was 'convicted of mischievous teaching and expelled from the Christian community'.[12] Talmage would have done well to ponder the preface to Eusebius's *History*, for the author states, as one of the purposes of his work, to set out the 'names and dates of those who, through a passion for innovation, have wandered as far as possible from the truth'.

Another declared purpose of Eusebius was to trace the apostolic succession. Here we touch upon the one sure test of orthodoxy. Throughout this work Eusebius is at pains to distinguish true and erroneous teachings; and he is in no doubt as to the criteria one should apply. Phrases such as 'built on the foundations of the churches everywhere laid by the apostles', and 'whose transmission of the apostolic teaching' soon acquire a familiar ring. Eusebius recalls that when Ignatius of Antioch was on his way to Rome and martyrdom, he gave encouragement to the Christian communities in every city where he stayed, warning them against heresy and, as an antidote, exhorting them to hold fast to the apostolic tradition. After listing a number of writers, most of them bishops, who flourished in the Church in the second century, Eusebius adds: 'In every case writings which show their orthodoxy and unshakeable devotion to the apostolic tradition have come into my hands.'[13] He then goes on to mention their works. The concept of apostolic tradition, regarded as the supreme test of orthodoxy, was applied to documents to distinguish the authentic from those of dubious origin. Arguing against the authenticity of certain books attributed to Clement of Rome, Eusebius urges two objections: first, there is no mention of them by early writers, and secondly, they do not 'preserve in its purity the stamp of apostolic orthodoxy'.[14]

If we are to inquire where this apostolic tradition resided, we will see that it was centred in the episcopacy. Talmage was guilty of selective quotation when citing Hegesippus' catalogue of heresies. He ought to have read the foregoing paragraph, where Hegesippus has this to say:

> On arrival at Rome I pieced together the succession down to Anicetus, whose deacon was Eleutherus, Anicetus being succeeded by Soter and he by Eleutherus. *In every line of bishops and in every city things accord with the preaching of the Law, the Prophets, and the Lord.*[15]

The apostolic succession was perpetuated in the bishops of the churches founded by the apostles. The bishops were the authorised teachers and custodians of the Faith, for they derived their authority and powers from the Apostles.

Mormons contend that there was no apostolic succession and that the authority of the Apostles ended with the death of St John. Their blindness in the face of the evidence is partly accounted for by their ignorance of Church history. But their principal difficulty is due to their peculiar fascination for numbers. We have already seen how, on the basis of a solitary text, Mormons established an office known as the Seventy. Their problem is stated by Talmage in *The Great Apostasy*: 'We have no evidence that the presiding council of the Church, comprising the twelve apostles, was continued beyond the earthly ministry of those who had been ordained to this holy calling during the life of Christ or soon after his ascension.'[16] The number twelve, then, is the stumbling block. Numbers had symbolic meaning for the Jews. Symbolically, there were twelve apostles, as there were twelve tribes of Israel. The gentile nations were thought to number seventy or seventy-two. True, Matthias was elected to replace Judas in making up the Twelve; but the Christian Church had not progressed beyond Jerusalem at the time. As the Church expanded to embrace gentiles, certain Jewish features, circumcision, for example, were set aside. The numbers twelve and seventy were meaningful in the Jewish context. But Christianity is a world faith: there was no intrinsic reason why the number of the Apostles' successors at any one time should be restricted to twelve. What mattered was that the Apostles' authority should be handed on; and this, we know, was done.

The written evidence clearly shows this. We have already referred to Hegesippus. The appeal to a living, apostolic tradition is nowhere better stated than by Irenaeus in *Heresies Answered*.

> Those that wish to discern the truth may observe the apostolic tradition made manifest in every church throughout the world. We can enumerate those who were appointed bishops in the churches by the Apostles, and their successors down to our own day, who never taught, and never knew, absurdities such as these men produce. For if the Apostles had known hidden mysteries... they would rather have committed them to those to whom they entrusted the churches. For they wished those men to be perfect and unblameable whom they left as their successors and to whom they handed over their own office authority.

Irenaeus had a direct link with the Apostolic age, for he was a disciple of Polycarp, who was a disciple of St John the Apostle. After recording the succession of the bishops of Rome down to his own time, Irenaeus pens this tribute to Polycarp I.[17]

> And then Polycarp, besides being instructed by the Apostles and acquainted with many who had seen the Lord, was also appointed by the Apostles for Asia as bishop of the Church in Smyrna. Even I saw him in my early youth; for he remained with us a long time... and departed this life, having taught always the things which he had learnt from the Apostles, which the Church hands down, which alone are true. There testify to these things all the churches throughout Asia, and the successors of Polycarp down to

this day, testimonies to the truth far more trustworthy and reliable than Valentinus and Marcion and the other misguided persons.[18]

Tertullian, a second century African lawyer, controversialist and scholar, has left us with one of the clearest statements on tradition and succession.

> But if any of these (heresies) are bold enough to insert themselves into the Apostolic age, in order to seem to have been handed down from the Apostles because they existed under the Apostles, we can say: Let them then produce the origins of their churches; let them unroll the list of their bishops, an unbroken succession from the beginning so that first bishop had as his precursor and the source of his authority one of the Apostles or one of the apostolic men who, though not an Apostle, continued with the Apostles. This is how the apostolic churches report their origins; thus the church of the Smyrnaeans relates that Polycarp was appointed by John, the church of Rome that Clement was ordained by Peter....[19]

Could anything be plainer than that? Could it be possible to have more convincing testimonies to the reality of the apostolic succession than those we have just cited?

As we might expect, the bishops were the great champions of orthodoxy, and we can now show them exercising their apostolic office in opposition to heresy. So we find Irenaeus of Lyons in his aforementioned work detailing the errors of the Gnostics. Irenaeus also, together with Bishops Dionysius of Corinth, Theophilus of Antioch, Philip of Gortyna, and Hippolytus (whose see is unknown) took issue with Marcion. Novatian, Nepos and Sabellius all found a worthy opponent in Dionysius, Bishop of Alexandria. Serapion was among many who opposed Montanus and his followers. Though not himself a bishop, his letter contained the signatures of several.

These were individual efforts: there is ample proof of concerted action on the part of the bishops. A large synod convened at Rome to consider the views of Novatian, who held that those Christians who had weakened during the persecution of the emperor Decius and had offered pagan sacrifices were beyond salvation. The synod, Eusebius says, was attended by sixty bishops. Bishops not present wrote assenting to the decision taken. Novatian and his followers were condemned, and it was decreed that 'those brothers who had had the misfortune to fall should be treated and cured with the medicine of repentance'.[20]

Paul of Samosata was condemned by a large gathering of bishops who met in a synod at Antioch. Eusebius mentions some of them, and reproduces the letter drafted by the bishops expressing their united judgement, addressed to the bishops of Rome and Alexandria and despatched to all provinces of the Empire.[21] Amazingly, this gathering of the bishops in synod in defence of orthodoxy is seen by Mormons as further evidence of apostasy.[22] In Mormon logic, the disease, the body it attacks, and the medicine for recovery are all one and the same.

The literature of the period, then, is replete with proofs that heresy was met and ably refuted by the bishops of the churches, singly and in concert in the exercise of their office as successors of the Apostles, and in fulfilment of Christ's promise that the powers of death would never prevail against his Church.[23]

Mormon double standards

Taking the apostasy argument a stage further, Mormons charge the Christian Church with becoming increasingly and incurably corrupt. They see this manifested in the personal lives of the clergy, especially the popes, and in the political ambitions of the papacy. Talmage and others scan the centuries to uncover the sordid details. Every unworthy pope and cleric is paraded for our disapprobation: every scandal and political intrigue becomes grist to the mill. Let a prince or emperor meddle in Church affairs, or a pontiff engage in affairs of state, and you have irrefutable proof that the Church was hopelessly corrupt.

This black legend of the Mormon view of history betrays at bottom a misconception regarding the nature of Christ's Church. Israel was often unfaithful to the Covenant — hence the need of prophets. The history of the monarchy reveals a catalogue of crimes of idolatry, murder and oppression. Yet Old Testament kings were revered as being next to God. They were anointed for their office, that is, set apart as sacred. Some of the Bible's most honoured personalities had moral flaws. King David arranged the murder of Uriah, yet his memory was held sacred by the Jews. Bartimaeus hailed Jesus as 'Son of David',[24] an act which amounted to an acknowledgement of Jesus as Messiah.

From among his many followers Jesus chose the Twelve. One of these betrayed him; another, at a critical moment, denied all knowledge of him, and all twelve deserted him when he needed them most. Yet it was upon these same men, only Judas excepted, that Christ founded his Church. The Bible is full of examples of weak men. The Book of Mormon by contrast knows only good and bad people. The human condition delineated in the Bible is present throughout history. Search the pages of history for immoral clerics and of course you will find them. That only proves that clerics are human.

Inherent in Mormonism is the conviction that Christianity failed. Mormons, consequently, see only the dark side of history. Yet the papacy which was dominated by the patrician families of Rome in the tenth century, was invigorated in the two succeeding centuries by the spirit, first of Cluny, then of Citeaux. The worldly popes of the Renaissance gave place to a whole line of reforming popes of the Counter-Reformation. In every age the Church could boast countless members of outstanding sanctity. These facts are never reported by Mormons: they do not fit their view of history.

The allegation that there are blots on the Church's record cannot and need not be denied. Christ likened his Church to a net cast into a sea containing both good and bad fish;[25] the Fathers of the Second Vatican Council described the Church as being 'at the same time holy and always in need of being purified'.[26] Human frailty, a conspicuous fact in the history of Mormonism, is a curious blind spot with Mormons when dwelling on their opponents' shortcomings.

It seemed necessary to expose the weakness in the line of argument adopted by Mormons. There is no need, however, to answer the charge of immorality, for it has already been done for us; by Brigham Young, no less. When once relating the moral failings of the young Joseph Smith, Brigham Young concluded with these words: 'That he was all of these things is nothing against his mission. God can and does make use of the vilest instruments'.[27] A more striking and, from the Mormon side, authoritative statement on the distinction between the person and the office would be hard to come by. In a single pithy sentence the great Mormon leader has demolished the charge levelled by Mormon writers against unworthy popes and clerics.

That Mormons should accuse the Church of political involvement is quite staggering in its audacity. Not that the accusation can be denied. But the leadership of Mormonism had from the outset a strong political motivation. The Mormon historian, B.H. Roberts, records that the Zion brethren accused Joseph Smith of 'seeking after monarchial power and authority'.[28] Even Cowdery charged him with attempting to set up a government within a government, to be controlled by the Mormon Church.[29] Parley Pratt, a contemporary of Joseph Smith and a writer held in high regard by Mormons, argued quite forcefully that the Mormon Church and the government and institutions of the United States were inseparable.[30] Joseph Smith's younger brother, William, though a High Priest of the

Mormon Church and one of its Twelve Apostles, was for a time a member of the House of Representatives of the Legislature of Illinois. Yet this combining of high ecclesiastical and political office is precisely what Mormons profess to find so objectionable in orthodox Christianity.

Then, Mormons conveniently forget that Joseph Smith, Prophet and first Elder of the Church, allowed himself to be put forward as a candidate for the highest political office in the land — the presidency of the United States.[31] Sidney Rigdon was to have been his Vice-President. Smith even issued a manifesto offering his solution to the nation's ills. But none of this compares with the actions of the Mormon authorities in Utah in 1890 when, in order to obtain statehood for their territory, they officially repudiated the practice of polygamy, enshrined in *Doctrine and Covenants* as a command having divine sanction. Thus was Mormon dogma sacrificed on the altar of political expediency.

It is highly instructive, bearing in mind the charge of apostasy which has been directed against the Christian Church, to inquire more closely into the nature of the alleged restoration. Ironically, within a few short years of its foundation, the Mormon Church was rent with discord in both its Ohio and Missouri settlements. Mormon historians do not shirk the task of recording the sorry events. Roberts tells of 'vexatious law suits' among the Saints of Far West, Missouri, and of systematic efforts 'to undermine and destroy the influence of the presidency of the church'.[32] Opposition to Joseph Smith was so intense among the Kirtland brethren at one stage that no one could safely defend him. Brigham Young was obliged to flee Kirtland in the December of 1837 because 'he continued to proclaim publicly that Joseph Smith was a prophet of the Most High and had not transgressed and fallen, as the apostates declared'.[33] The following year matters worsened, many more brethren demonstrating their hostility to Joseph Smith.

At this point it might well be asked: what was the reaction of Mormon officialdom to the onslaughts directed against the restored Church? Do we find the religious authorities presenting a united front in opposition to heresy, as was the case with the bishops in the early Church? Sadly, the highest authorities in the Mormon Church were themselves divided. Some remained loyal to Smith; but many rejected him. In Kirtland, Ohio, Roberts informs us, there was no quorum of the Church free from apostasy. An attempt was made by members of the leading councils of the Kirtland church to depose Joseph Smith. They included Warren Parish of the Seventy, and John F. Boynton and Luke S. Johnson of the Quorum of the Twelve Apostles.[34] In

1838 John Whitmer, W.W. Phelps, Lyman E. Johnson and William E. McLellin were all excommunicated, and Oliver Cowdery and David Whitmer anticipated their excommunication in letters announcing their withdrawal from the Church. Every one of these men held high ecclesiastical office. The Whitmers and Phelps occupied the presidency of the Church in Missouri. Cowdery occupied a position in the Church second only to Joseph Smith, while Johnson and McLellin were members of the quorum of the Twelve Apostles. John Whitmer was also the official Church historian. Roberts tells how he refused to hand over the Church records when he was deposed.

In February 1835 the Council of the Twelve Apostles had been chosen in fulfilment of a revelation said to have been made to Joseph Smith. Of the original twelve, eight either lapsed or were excommunicated, though four of these were later restored to membership of the Church. William Smith, the Prophet's brother and one of the Twelve, was excommunicated, re-admitted, and excommunicated a second time in the course of a stormy career that found him frequently at odds with his brother.[35]

To appreciate the seriousness of these defections one must understand that, as the Apostles of the Restored Church, these men allegedly possessed the same spiritual powers as Christ's Apostles. To suppose a parallel situation in the twelve appointed by Christ, one might imagine that only four remained faithful to their office. The implications suggested by the analogy are staggering. The issue of apostolic succession in the early Church would indeed be problematical if two thirds of the apostolic college had apostasised within a few years of its institution. However, the early Church was assailed from without, and successfully defended. The first decade of its existence saw Mormonism disintegrating at the core. We can now appreciate with what mind-boggling effrontery Mormons project the failings of Mormonism onto orthodox Christianity. Such was the condition of the Mormon Church in Joseph Smith's lifetime. Matters worsened after his death, when it broke up into numerous groups, each with its own leadership, and each claiming lawful succession from Joseph Smith. One church was set up at Kirtland with David Whitmer as prophet. Lyman Wight took a group to Texas, while Sidney Rigdon, who had been excommunicated in Nauvoo, established a church in Pennsylvania. There were many others, some of the splinter groups themselves having off-shoots. Most were insignificant, destined soon to become extinct.[36]

Today, apart from the Utah or Brighamite Mormons, the one other church of any size and importance is the Reorganized

Church of Jesus Christ of Latter-day Saints, with its headquarters in Independence (Zion) Missouri. This Church sprang up around Emma Smith, Joseph's widow, and secured the allegiance of most of Joseph Smith's family. It claims to be the true Church by reason of lineal descent from the Prophet. The legality of the claim has been upheld in the courts. Between these two main bodies, the Brighamites and the Reorganized Church, there is considerable disagreement over fundamentals.

8

Mormon Doctrine

To say that Mormon doctrine developed can be misleading. The religion of the Book of Mormon reflects the biblical, Protestant ethos of Joseph Smith's early youth. Once Smith had gained acceptance as a prophet, his religious thinking became increasingly deviant and confused, later additions to the content of faith not infrequently contradicting what had gone before.

God
In its teaching on the Godhead, the Book of Mormon is strictly monotheistic. The unity of God is common knowledge to all the Nephite prophets. The first of these, Nephi, writing about 600 BC, records the appearance of an angel who came proclaiming: 'There is one God and one Shepherd over all the earth' *(1 Nephi 13:41).* A few centuries later the prophet Mosiah uttered this exhortation:

> Believe in God: believe that he is,
> and that he created all things, both
> in heaven and on earth; believe that
> man doth not comprehend all the
> things which the Lord can comprehend *(Mosiah 4:9).*

Even the ancient Jaredites were monotheists, when their contemporaries at their place of origin in the Old World paid worship to a pantheon of more than 500 gods.[1] Their scribe, Ether, records that when God led the Jaredites to the land of promise he made it a condition that they 'from that time henceforth and forever, should serve him, the true and only God' *(Ether 2:8).*

The monotheism of the Book of Mormon prophets is preserved in the early sections of *Doctrine and Covenants*. Section 20, verse 19 is virtually identical with the foregoing verse from the Book of Ether:

> And gave unto them commandments
> that they should love and serve
> him, the only living and true God.

This is taken from the text of a revelation which Joseph Smith recorded in April 1830. Some time afterwards, Smith began a study of Hebrew, during the course of which he discovered that the Hebrew word for God, Elohim, was in the plural form. Thereafter, Smith's 'revelations' regarding the nature of God were unmistakably polytheistic. In section 121, verse 32 we read:

> According to that which was
> ordained in the midst of the Council
> of the Eternal God of all other gods
> before this world was.

This new direction in Mormon theology culminates in chapters 4 and 5 of the Book of Abraham, a division of the *Pearl of Great Price*, in which the first two chapters of Genesis are re-written to give a polytheistic version of the creation story. Wherever the Bible account speaks of God, Joseph Smith substitutes 'the gods'. The more elaborated religion of Mormonism, then, is thoroughly polytheistic, in contrast with the monotheism of the Book of Mormon. From the outset, the Reorganized Church rejected the Book of Abraham and the doctrine of the plurality of gods, holding that Joseph Smith was experiencing a temporary lapse from prophetic office when he taught it.[2]

The Mormon doctrine of God is also crudely anthropomorphic. Mormons infer from Genesis 1:26 — 'Let us make man in Our image' — that God is tangible, possessing bodily parts. *Doctrine and Covenants*, proclaims in section 130: 'The Father has a body of flesh and bones as tangible as man's'. George Edward Clark insists that God has a face because Exodus 33:11 records that He spoke to Moses face to face. Clark then turns his attention to verse 23 — 'You shall see my back: but my face shall not be seen'. This verse, Clark explains, 'informs us that Moses could not see God's face, but did see his "back parts" '.[3]

Gordon H. Fraser has something to say about this type of kindergarten theology in his book, *Is Mormonism Christian?* 'The phrase ''face to face'' is the Hebrew expression conveying intimacy between Moses and God. The Bible is full of such antropomorphisms. This does not imply that God is corporeal but indicates that He communicated Himself in expressions with which men were familiar.... The only difficulty here is in the paucity of human language.'[4] Fraser then charges Joseph Smith with failing to understand the significance of scriptural language and values. In this regard, Smith set a precedent that has been faithfully observed by Mormon commentators who have followed him.

Christ

Mormon teaching about Christ must be seen in the context of the doctrine of the pre-existence of spirits. Put simply, all mortals existed in heaven in spirit from before their earthly existence — 'Man was also in the beginning with God' (*Doctrine and Covenants* 93:29). Not only humanity, but all living things of earth had a pre-existence in the spirit. Talmage calls it a 'primeval childhood or first estate'. The doctrine is nowhere taught in the Book of Mormon, but became current very early in the Mormon Church. The fullest statement of the doctrine in Mormon scripture occurs in the *Pearl of Great Price,* in Moses 3:5:

> For I, the Lord God, created
> all things, of which I have spoken,
> spiritually, before they were naturally
> upon the face of the earth... And
> I, the Lord, God, had created all
> the children of men; and not yet
> a man to till the ground; for in
> heaven created I them; and there
> was not yet flesh upon the earth,
> neither in the water, neither in the air.

Christ, seemingly, was only one of these spirit children of the Father. He was the firstborn of the sons and daughters of Elohim.[5] We are his juniors in the order of spirit creation. 'There is no impropriety', writes Talmage, 'in speaking of Jesus Christ as the Elder Brother of the rest of human kind.'[6] Moreover, in his mortal life Christ was conceived in the normal way, though in the matter of his parentage he was unlike other mortals. His father in the flesh was a resurrected and glorified being, whom Brigham Young has identified as Adam, who is also Michael the Archangel and God the Father.[7]

Christ differs from us in two other respects — in his pre-ordination as our Saviour, and in his sinlessness.[8] Still, this falls far short of the Christian estimation of Christ as the incarnate Son of God, co-equal and co-eternal with the Father.[9] Being the God-man, Christ is able to atone for sin and effect the reconciliation of God and humanity. For, as God, his every act has supreme value: as man, he acts for us; he is the representative human. The act by which Christ atoned for sin and restored us to friendship with God was his crucifixion and death on the cross. 'For Christ also died for sins once for all, the righteous for the unrighteous, that he might bring us to God' *(1 Peter 3:18)*. However, if Christ is only our 'elder brother' and not God-made-man, there can be no atonement: Christ's death on the Cross loses its efficacy, and our salvation is not assured.

The Trinity

Like orthodox Christians, Mormons profess a belief in a triune God. The first of their Articles of Faith states:

> We believe in God, the Eternal Father, and
> in His Son, Jesus Christ, and in the Holy Ghost.

Doctrine and Covenants, section 20, verse 28 adds:

> Which Father, Son and Holy Ghost are one God,
> infinite and eternal, without end.

So far, so good. The point of disagreement is reached when Mormons attempt to define the nature of the Persons of the Trinity and their relationship to one another. As we have seen, Mormons believe that God the Father has a body of flesh and bones. We pause in observing the inconsistency of believing in a God who is infinite, without limits, who nevertheless possesses that most limiting thing, a material body. Their teaching on the Holy Ghost is obscure. Clark says: 'The exact nature of the Holy Ghost — how He can be a personage of Spirit dwelling in a spirit body — is not fully comprehended by mortal men.'[10] Yet it is obvious that Mormons can contemplate no mode of being other than the material. Spirit bodies, it seems, are of the substance of matter. *Doctrine and Covenants*, section 131, verse 7, states:

> All spirit is matter, but it
> is more fine or pure, and
> can only be discerned by
> purer eyes.

Talmage declares an immaterial being to be a contradiction in terms. Writing on the Trinity, he says: 'That these three are separate individuals, physically distinct from each other, is demonstrated by the accepted records of divine dealings with man.'[11] LeGrand Richards also argues that the three persons of the Trinity can only be distinguished by supposing that each possesses a physical body.[12] The absence of body parts, he believes, renders God 'incomprehensible'.[13]

If the Father, Son and Holy Ghost are physically distinct from one another, in what sense are they one God? Talmage provides the answer: 'The Godhead is a type of unity in the attributes, powers, and purposes of its members.'[14] But this does not mean that the Father, Son and Holy Ghost are one in substance, for Talmage categorically denies it. What emerges here is the belief in a deity composed of three quite separate gods.

Humankind

Mormon doctrine was given a new twist when, shortly before his own death, Joseph Smith delivered a funeral oration for Elder King Follett. Before a congregation of 20,000 Mormons, Smith proclaimed: 'God was once as we are now, and is an exalted man'. The doctrine was later expressed by Lorenzo Snow in an epigram that has become famous: 'As man is, God once was. As God is now, man may become'. The polytheism we have noted in the Mormon doctrine of God is here indicated as a logical consequence of the Mormon 'doctrine of man'. When, therefore, Mormons pray to God the Father, they are addressing merely the first of many gods who, having once inhabited the earth as mortals, now inhabit the heavens as resurrected and glorified beings. Mormonism thus exalts man as embryonic god, while diminishing God as defined man.

Once God becomes God he is not the immutable being of Malachi 3:6 — 'For I the Lord do not change'. For God is part of a plan of progression that involves the whole of nature. He is constantly evolving. Though perfect, he possesses, says Talmage, 'this essential quality of true perfection — the capacity of eternal increase'.[15] Those of us who have thought that perfection is that to which nothing can be added, might be excused for finding Talmage's aphorism somewhat lacking in logic.

Since man is himself evolving towards Godhood, will he eventually be the equal of the God he worships? No, says Talmage, for 'to assert such would be to argue that there is no progression beyond a certain stage of attainment, and that advancement is a characteristic of low organisation and inferior purpose alone'.[16] Evolution, then, is a handicap event, with God and man covering the same course, but God having an early start and always remaining in front.

That the notion of a changeable God is at variance with what the Bible teaches, is only what we should expect. It is also at variance with the teaching of the Book of Mormon. A few examples from the many passages that could be cited will make the point sufficiently clear.

> For do we not read that God
> is the same yesterday, today and
> forever, and in him there is no
> variableness neither shadow
> of changing? *(Mormon 9:9)*

> And behold, I say unto you he
> changeth not; if so he would
> cease to be God. *(Mormon 9:19)*

> For I know that God is not a
> partial God, neither a changeable
> being; but he is unchangeable
> from all eternity to all eternity.
>
> *(Moroni 8:18)*

We are surely only being fair in demanding that Mormons reconcile the God of 'eternal increase' of their later theology, with the immutable God of the Book of Mormon, even if it should seem like an exercise in reconciling the irreconcilable.

Baptism

In common with the Christian Churches, Mormonism attaches great importance to baptism. Indeed, the divine destiny of humanity depends on it.

Mormons know only one baptism, the baptism of John the Baptist. On this matter Mormon writers are emphatic. On pages 79-81 of his book, *Why I Believe*, George Edward Clark supports his discussion of the subject with quotations from the gospels, Acts and St Paul, making no distinction between John's baptism and that instituted by Christ.[17] It was John's baptism that St Peter administered to Cornelius, according to LeGrand Richards.[18] Elsewhere, Richards remarks: 'There is only one baptism, and that is John's baptism'.[19] Typically, it was said to be at the direction of John the Baptist that Joseph Smith and Oliver Cowdery administered the rite to each other. Mormons accordingly insist on total immersion as the only valid means of administration.

According to Mormon belief, the special purpose of baptism

is to afford entry into Christ's Church with remission of sins.[20]
This presents a difficulty if the only baptism is John's baptism.
For at the time that John was baptising in the River Jordan,
Christ's Church was a thing of the future. How, one wonders,
was it possible to be baptised into a church that didn't then exist?
John's baptism was a symbol of repentance for the forgiveness
of sins. It was not Christian baptism. It did not give the Holy
Spirit. Although John appears in the New Testament, he is
generally regarded as being the last in the tradition of Old
Testament prophets. His baptism should not be seen on a merely
personal level but, true to the prophetic tradition, as a call to
repentance for the sins of the nation.[21]

That John's baptism did not give the Holy Spirit, he himself
made clear: 'After me comes he who is mightier that I, the thong
of whose sandals I am not worthy to stoop down and untie. I
have baptised you with water; but he will baptise you with the
Holy Spirit' *(Mark 1:7-8)*.

The point is reinforced by events at Ephesus. St Luke, the author
of Acts, tells of Appolos, a Jew who preached about Jesus,
'though he knew only the baptism of John'.[22] When St Paul
arrived at Ephesus, he re-baptised a number of disciples who had
earlier received John's baptism:

> And he said to them,
> 'Did you receive the Holy Spirit when
> you believed?' And they said,
> 'No, we have never even heard
> that there is a Holy Spirit.' And
> he said, 'Into what then were
> you baptised?' They said, 'Into
> John's baptism.' And Paul said,
> 'John baptised with the baptism
> of repentance, telling the people
> to believe in the one who was
> to come after him, that is, Jesus.'
> On hearing this, they were
> baptised in the name of the Lord Jesus.

(Acts 19:2-6)

Mormons reject infant baptism, but believe adult baptism to be
essential for salvation. *Doctrine and Covenants* 112:29 states:

> And he that believeth and is
> baptized shall be saved, and he
> that believeth not, and is not
> baptized, shall be damned.

To rescue from damnation the countless numbers of people who had died unbaptised, the Mormon Church introduced the doctrine of baptism for the dead. This enables Mormons to undergo proxy baptisms on behalf of the dead. The doctrine is based on 1 Corinthians 15:29, in which St Paul mentions the practice of vicarious baptism for the dead without approving it.

Acceptance of the gospel being a prerequisite if damnation is to be avoided, Mormon teaching makes no allowance for sincere unbelievers. They, in common with unrepentant sinners, must suffer endless torment — according to the Book of Mormon, that is.[23] However, the unmitigated teaching of the Book of Mormon on eternal punishment is softened in *Doctrine and Covenants* by a most ingenious piece of sophistry, to the conclusion that it is for a time only. The damned are granted a second chance to repent of their sins and accept the gospel, with the possibility of inhabiting a lesser heaven.

Celestial marriage

No religion places greater emphasis on marriage than Mormonism which teaches that marriage is a solemn agreement which extends beyond the grave for all eternity. Marriage, the home and procreation are facts of life in heaven, as on earth.

The teaching goes far beyond that, however. In this scheme the human person is incomplete unless married. Only those who have entered into the married state, and have had their marriages sealed in Mormon Temples, can hope to achieve celestial glory, the highest of the three degrees of glory in the next world.[24] Further, the blessings of eternal marriage depend upon ordination to the Melchisedek Priesthood,[25] consequently only ordained Mormons can aspire to places in the highest heaven, that is to godhood.[26] Unmarried people and those whose marriages have not been sealed in Mormon Temples, if baptised, become angels in the next world.

Eternal marriage is such an integral part of Mormon doctrine that even God the Father must have a female counterpart, the 'mother of spirits'.[27] We will search the Bible in vain for anything remotely resembling teaching such as this. LeGrand Richards admits that the Mormon dogma of celestial marriage comes not from the Bible, but from private revelations made to Joseph Smith.[28]

It is interesting to speculate on the implications of this teaching. The argument assumes that all marriages are happy marriages. But even good Mormons must sometimes contract bad marriages. It is little comfort to the man tied to a disagreeable wife, or to the wife of a brutish man, to be told that their union endures beyond the grave and for all eternity. The system also offends against our sense of justice, when the highest bliss of heaven depends, not on a virtuous life, but on the individual's marital status. On this reckoning St Paul, not having married, would be undeserving of celestial glory, whereas the average sinner would be worthy of godhood if his marriage had been sealed in a Mormon Temple.

Even more intriguing is the place of Christ in such a scheme. Since being married for eternity in this world is the necessary condition of godhood in the next, will we enjoy celestial glory while our Redeemer occupies a lesser heaven? Mormons manage to avoid this absurdity with a solution equally absurd, if not blasphemous. They say that Christ was married. The Mormon theologian, Orson Hyde, alleges that at the marriage at Cana Christ was the groom, and 'took unto him Mary, Martha and the other Mary' as his wives.[29] He further asserts that Christ had issue: 'I shall say here that before the Saviour died He looked upon His own natural children as we look upon ours'.[30] Christian sensibilities recoil from such views. Needless to say, they are wholly unscriptural.

Christ leaves no doubt that marriage is of earthly duration and does not survive the grave. This emerges in his disputation with the Sadducees.[31] The Sadducees were a Jewish party who did not believe in the future life. A number of them put to Christ the hypothetical case of a woman who married seven brothers in turn, each one dying in her lifetime. The Sadducees' question was, to which of the seven would she be a wife in the future life, since all seven had been husband to her in this life. Christ's reply, in effect, was to tell the Sadducees that their question was irrelevant, for marriage is a state of mortal life only:

> You are wrong because you
> know neither the scriptures
> nor the power of God. For
> in the resurrection they neither
> marry nor are given in marriage
> but are like angels in heaven.[32]

Since procreation is so important in the next life, we can appreciate why Mormons incline to polygamy, for clearly the more wives a man has, the greater will be his progeny. The doctrine is set forth in Section 132 of *Doctrine and Covenants*. Joseph Smith's wife, Emma, is commanded to acquiesce in his taking plural wives:

> And let mine handmaid,
> Emma Smith, receive all
> those that have been given
> unto my servant, Joseph.

The example of the patriarchs and of David and Solomon is cited as additional proof that the doctrine is scriptural.

Once again we are compelled to note that peculiarity of Mormonism which permits one volume of scripture to teach a doctrine that another volume of scripture repudiates. Fewer evils have been condemned more forthrightly in the Book of Mormon than that of polygamy. A few examples will show how abhorrent the practice was made to appear to the Nephite prophets, and in what unequivocal language it was denounced:

> Behold, David and Solomon
> truly had many wives and
> concubines, which thing was
> abominable before me, saith
> the Lord. *(Jacob 2:24)*

> Wherefore my brethren, hear me,
> and hearken to the word of the Lord:
> For there shall not any man
> among you have save it be
> one wife; and concubines he
> shall have none. *(Jacob 2:27)*

> And it came to pass that
> Riplakish did not do that
> which was right in the
> sight of the Lord, for he
> did have many wives
> and concubines. *(Ether 10:5)*

Section 132 of *Doctrine and Covenants* was recorded in 1843. Twelve years earlier Joseph Smith had received two revelations which are recorded as Sections 42 and 49. Section 42, verse 22 reads:

> Thou shalt love thy wife
> with all thy heart and shalt
> cleave unto her and none else.

Section 49, verse 16 reads:

> Wherefore it is lawful that
> he should have one wife,
> and they twain shall be one flesh.

It is quite evident, then, that, concerning the practice of polygamous marriages, not only is *Doctrine and Covenants* at variance with the teaching of the Book of Mormon, it is also at variance with itself.

Mormons of the Reorganized Church have never accepted Section 132 of *Doctrine and Covenants*. Neither do they accept the doctrine of celestial marriage.[33] But in acknowledging Joseph Smith, the author of Section 132, as God's prophet, they betray their inconsistency, and render their position no more tenable than that of the Brighamites.

Continuing revelation
Whereas most Christians believe the death of St John to have set the seal on the scriptures, Mormons are committed to a belief in the necessity of continuing revelation. The Bible has to be supplemented by additional scriptures, to be revealed whenever God deems it fitting. Were it not so, say Mormons, God would be abandoning the Church to its own devices.

Few revelations have been received in recent years. In the years when the Church was led by Joseph Smith, hardly any decisions were taken without guidance from above. This meant that many purely mundane matters were recorded in *Doctrine and Covenants* as divine revelation. God, through Joseph Smith, appointed committees, distributed offices, and gave instructions for the buying and selling of land for the building of houses, storehouses and printing works. In both spiritual and temporal matters the smallest contingency was answered by a revelation.

The contents of the *Pearl of Great Price* are hardly more profound, and belie the title of that work. The volume consists of the alleged writings of Moses and Abraham, Matthew 24 in the 'inspired' translation of Joseph Smith, thirteen pages of Smith's personal history, and the Church's Articles of Faith. Most of these writings have been referred to above. Because of the astonishing circumstances surrounding its discovery it is worth devoting a paragraph to the Book of Abraham.

Joseph Smith claimed to have translated the work from papyri which had formed part of the wrappings of Egyptian mummies belonging to a travelling showman named Chandler. On first sight of the papyri, Smith declared them to have been written by Abraham when he was in Egypt. However improbable this must have seemed, Smith was in little danger of contradiction, for ancient Egyptian was then an unknown language. The *Pearl of Great Price* contains reproductions from the papyri with Joseph Smith's interpretations. These have been examined in recent times by several of the most eminent Egyptologists and Smith's interpretations have been found to be wholly incorrect. All agree that the papyri are nothing more than the ordinary funerary texts common to ancient Egypt, though not common until long after Abraham's time.[34]

Against the Mormon belief in continuing revelation can be set the plain teaching of the New Testament that the fullness of revelation is to be found in and through the person of Jesus Christ. Christ said: 'I am the way, and the truth, and the life' *(John 14:6)*. Not 'I have', but 'I am'. It is the person of Christ, then, that interests us. But Christ claimed to be one with the Father (John 10:30). To know Christ, therefore, is to know the Father. He also said: 'All that I have heard from my Father I have made known to you' *(John 15:15)*. Clearly this makes additional revelations and further covenants superfluous. One might gain clearer insights into the Christian revelation by study and meditation, but one cannot add to it. Christ is all-sufficient.

As to the assertion that without supplementary scriptures Christ's Church would be left abandoned, we have Christ's personal guarantee that this will never happen. For when his earthly ministry was accomplished, Christ drew his Apostles to a mountain in Galilee: there he invested them with his own authority, commanding them to teach and baptise all nations, and sent them forth from that place into the world with a promise ringing in their ears:

I am with you always, to
the close of the age (*Matthew 28:20*).

Conclusion

What then must be the verdict on Mormonism? Was Joseph Smith, money-digger and convicted charlatan, worthy of belief when he claimed to have discovered gold plates buried in the earth? Were Smith's witnesses really the kind of sober-minded men whose judgement in matters respecting the supernatural can be relied on? Does the evidence support the contention that the *Book of Mormon* is the religious and historical record of ancient America, or does it disprove it? Finally, does Mormonism truly represent a latter-day revelation for humankind? Is it not rather a travesty of Christianity, its teachings the bizarre outpourings of an imagination run riot? The issues are clear, the conclusion hardly in doubt. Where a critical faculty is lacking, the evidence for Mormonism might sometimes seem persuasive. Probe beneath the surface, however, and it is seen to be superficial, facile, and in every sense unscientific.

Notes

Introduction

1. LeGrand Richards, *A Marvelous Work and a Wonder,* pp. 397-8.

Part I — The Prophet

Chapter 1: The Mormon story

1. Lucy Mack Smith, *History of Joseph Smith,* chapters 13, 16 and 17.
2. See chapter 2.
3. The subject matter of the Book of Mormon will receive more detailed treatment in chapter 3.
4. *Doctrine and Covenants,* section 57.
5. Joseph Smith produced his own version of the Bible, which he claimed to have translated by 'inspiration'.
6. *Doctrine and Covenants,* section 132.
7. Joseph Smith's many wives have been documented by Fawn M. Brodie in an appendix to her biography of Smith, *No Man Knows My History.*

CHAPTER 2: The Mormon Story — A Critical Appraisal

1. The full text of the letter may be read in the well-documented *The Maze of Mormonism,* by W.R. Martin; Also in Volume 1 of *A Comprehensive History of the Church of Jesus Christ of Latter-day Saints* by Mormon historian, B.H. Roberts.
2. Ibid.
3. Mormon 9: 32, 34.
4. Hiram Page was married to one of the Whitmer girls.
5. LeGrand Richards, *A Marvelous Work and a Wonder,* p. 55.
6. Gordon B. Hinckley, *Truth Restored,* p. 28.
7. Fawn M. Brodie, *No Man Knows My History,* p. 81.
8. *History of Joseph Smith the Prophet By His Mother,* p. 139.

9. Joseph Fielding Smith, *Essentials in Church History*, p. 94.
10. Lucy Mack Smith, op.cit., pp. 241-3. See also Brodie, op. cit., p. 205.
11. *Defense in a Rehearsal of My Grounds for Separating Myself from the Latter Day Saints*, quoted in Brodie, op. cit., p. 73.
12. op. cit., Appendix A.
13. Thomas O'Dea, *The Mormons*, p. 6.
14. *Gleanings by the Way*, p. 225, quoted in W.R. Martin, *The Maze of Mormonism*, p. 19.
15. quoted in W.R. Martin, ibid., p. 26.
16. J. Oswald Sanders, *Heresies Ancient and Modern*, p. 106.
17. Brodie, op. cit., p. 17.
18. Used as a textbook in the training of Mormon missionaries.
19. Op.cit., pp. 91-2.
20. *History*, Century 1, Vol. 1, p. 82.
21. Ibid., p. 129.
22. Brodie, op. cit., Appendix A.
23. Ibid.
24. *No Ma'am, That's Not History*.
25. James Black, *New Forms of the Old Faith*, p. 249; the theory is discussed at length by Dr Black on pp. 248-9.
26. Op. cit., p. 47.
27. Lucy Mack Smith, op. cit., p. 83.

Part II — The Book

Chapter 3: Israelites in America

1. Robert Wauchope, *Lost Tribes and Sunken Continents*, chapters 2 and 3.
2. See especially 1 Nephi 12:3; Mormon 1:7; 3 Nephi 8:8-15, 24-25; 9:3-10; Ether 7:9; 9:23; 10:4,9,12; 14:17; 2 Nephi 5:15; Jarom 1:8; Alma 43:18-19; Ether 15:15; 10:23-27; 3 Nephi 6:8; Ether 9:17-19; 1 Nephi 18:25 .
3. Hunter and Ferguson, *Ancient America and the Book of Mormon*, pp. 14, 145-6; B.H. Roberts, *History*, Century 1, Vol. 1, p. 173.
4. *Archaeology and the Book of Mormon*, p. 25.
5. Quoted in James E. Talmage, *Articles of Faith*, pp. 292, 508.
6. Cited in Hunter, *Archaeology and the Book of Mormon*, pp. 44-45.
7. Cited in Hunter and Ferguson, *Ancient America and the Book of Mormon*, pp. 63-4.
8. Robert Wauchope, *Lost Tribes and Sunken Continents*, p. 63.
9. *Christ in Ancient America*, pp. 118-9.
10. Ibid, pp. 121-3.

CHAPTER 4: Are the Arguments Convincing?

1. 2 Nephi 5:21.
2. See, for example, G.H.S. Bushnell, *The First Americans*, pp. 34, 37-9.
3. *Red Man's America*, p. 1.

4. p. 21.
5. Robert Wauchope, *Lost Tribes and Sunken Continents*, p. 54.
6. Ibid.
7. New World pottery was produced by an alternative method: Bushnell, op. cit., pp. 8-9; Wauchope, *Handbook of Middle American Indians*, Vol. 1, p. 451.
8. On these matters see Wauchope, *Lost Tribes and Sunken Continents*, pp. 87-8; G. Daniel, *The First Civilizations*, pp. 161-2; R. Underhill, *Red Man's America*, p. 19.
9. This and the examples which follow are taken from Wauchope, *Lost Tribes and Sunken Continents*, chapter 7.
10. Josephy, op. cit., p. 23, *Encyclopaedia Britannica*, Vol. 1, article on American aboriginal languages.
11. Josephy, ibid.
12. Op. cit., p. 12.
13. *The Maya*, p. 30.
14. Op. cit., p. 23.
15. Wauchope, *Lost Tribes and Sunken Continents*, p. 62.
16. Daniel, *The First Civilizations*, Plate 63; see also Bushnell, *Ancient Arts of the Americas*, p. 28 and illustration on p. 29.
17. Coe, *Mexico*, p. 84.
18. Wauchope, op. cit., p. 62, and illustration facing p. 71.
19. Bushnell, *The First Americans*, p. 75 (italics mine).
20. Bushnell, ibid., p. 81, and *Ancient Arts of the Americas*, pp. 53-4. Sculptures from the two sites are among the illustrations to both of Dr Bushnell's books.
21. Bushnell, *The First Americans*, pp. 81-2.

Chapter 5: Archaeology and the Book of Mormon

1. *The First Civilizations*, p. 139
2. Their theories form the subject matter of Robert Wauchope's book, *Lost Tribes and Sunken Continents*.
3. The theory that the migrations took a West-to-East rather than an East-to-West direction is of more than passing interest, for Mormons subscribe to both views. The Book of Mormon relates how America was first settled by Jaredites who came from the Tower of Babel at the time of the confusion of languages and dispersal of the human race. But in *Doctrine and Covenants* Joseph Smith claims to have received a divine revelation naming Spring Hill, Missouri as the location of the Garden of Eden (Sections 116, 117 and 107, verse 53). Being stuck with two conflicting accounts of the origin of humanity disturbs the Mormons not at all. Talmage, in his *Articles of Faith*, upholds the first version on pp. 283-7 and the second on p. 474.
4. Coe, *Mexico*, pp. 31-2.
5. Talmage, *Articles of Faith*, p. 285; Clark, *Why I Believe*, p. 114.
6. Coe, *Mexico*, pp. 33-7; Underhill, *Red Man's America*, p. 9; Bushnell, *The First Americans*, p. 15.

7. Bushnell, ibid., p. 18.
8. Underhill, op. cit., p. 9.
9. Ibid., p. 11.
10. Bushnell, op. cit., p. 19.
11. Op. cit., p. 33.
12. *The First Civilizations*, p. 147.
13. p. 14.
14. The Wentworth Letter. See Clark, *Why I Believe*, p. 107. The Wentworth Letter was an early statement of Mormon belief made by Joseph Smith in response to a request from John Wentworth, Editor and proprietor of the *Chicago Democrat*. It is printed in full in Clark's book, pp. 105-111.
15. *Archaeology and the Book of Mormon*, p. 234.
16. *Christ in Ancient America*, p. 86.
17. Quoted in Daniel, *The First Civilizations*, p. 161.
18. Coe, *Mexico*, p. 104.
19. Daniel, op. cit., p. 133.
20. Ibid. p. 156; Bushnell, *Ancient Arts of the Americas*, p. 8; Underhill, *Red Man's America*, p. 19.
21. *The Indian Heritage of America*, p. 208.
22. Letter of the Smithsonian Institute, quoted in W.R. Martin, *The Maze of Mormonism*, p. 41.
23. Coe, *Mexico*, p. 24; Underhill, op. cit., pp. 18 and 20; Bushnell, *Ancient Arts of the Americas*, pp. 8-9; Wauchope, *Handbook of Middle American Indians*, Vol. 1, p. 456.
24. Martin, op. cit., p. 41; Underhill, op. cit., pp. 18-19; Wauchope, op. cit., p. 456, also *Lost Tribes and Sunken Continents*, p. 87.
25. Coe, op. cit., p. 24.
26. Wauchope, *Lost Tribes and Sunken Continents*, p. 87.
27. Ibid.
28. Coe, *Mexico*, p. 82; Daniel, op. cit., p. 159; Bushnell, *The First Americans*, p. 48.
29. Coe, op. cit., p. 103; Bushnell, op. cit., p. 59; Underhill, op. cit., p. 21.
30. *Progress and Religion*, p. 116.
31. Op. cit., p. 36.
32. *The Maya*, pp. 60-61.
33. Bushnell, op. cit., pp. 59-60.
34. Coe, *Mexico*, pp. 101-2.
35. Gordon Willey et al, *Handbook of Middle American Indians*, Vol. 1, Gen. ed. Robert Wauchope, pp. 459-460.
36. Josephy, *The Indian Heritage of America*, p. 203.
37. Coe, op. cit., pp. 109-110.
38. This was before the Lamanites supposedly changed Christ's name to Quetzalcoatl, so it cannot be said to be a symbolic representation of Christ.
39. Bushnell, *The First Americans*, p. 69.
40. Coe, *The Maya*, pp. 29-30; Daniel, *The First Civilizations*, p. 157.
41. Daniel, op. cit., p. 158; Coe, op. cit., p. 64.
42. *Ancient Arts of the Americas*, p. 36.
43. Ibid., p. 48; Coe, *Mexico*, p. 102.

44. Bushnell, op. cit., p. 104.
45. Op. cit., pp. 102-3.
46. Coe, *The Maya*, p. 52.
47. Coe, *Mexico*, p. 84.
48. See, for example, Bushnell, *Ancient Arts of the Americas*, pp. 22-3.
49. Josephy, *The Indian Heritage of America*, p. 199; Bushnell, *The First Americans*, p. 35.
50. Bushnell, op. cit., p. 40.
51. Ibid., p. 41.
52. The Wentworth Letter.
53. Coe, *Mexico*, p. 84.
54. See, for example, Bushnell, *The First Americans*, pp. 41-2.

Chapter 6: The Internal Evidence

1. Talmage, *Articles of Faith*, p. 505.
2. *Why I Believe*, p. 125.
3. 1 Kings 11:42.
4. The *King James Version*, that is.
5. See 1 Nephi 22:25; Mosiah 4:2,3;16:6; Alma 5:27, 38, 44, 48.
6. See 1 Nephi 10:7-10; 11:27, Alma 5:48.
7. S. Cook, *An Introduction to the Bible*, p. 57; A. Gelin, *The Religion of Israel*, pp. 71-2; E.W. Heaton, *The Old Testament Prophets*, pp. 83-9; W. Neil, *One-Volume Bible Commentary*, pp. 248 and 252.
8. See Moroni 7 and 10.
9. See Alma 16:13, Helaman 3:9,14.
10. *The Maze of Mormonism*, p. 44.
11. Ibid., p. 43.
12. Ibid., p. 44.
13. *The Vitality of Mormonism*, cited in A.A. Hoekema, *The Four Major Cults*, p. 18.
14. Pomeroy Tucker, *Origin, Rise and Progress of Mormonism*, ch. 11, quoted by Roberts in *History*, Vol. 1, p. 129.
15. *Address to All Believers in Christ*, p. 12, quoted in Roberts, op. cit., pp. 128 and 130.

Part III — The Cult

Chapter 7: A Restored Church?

1. *Articles of Faith*, p. 202.
2. *A Marvelous Work and a Wonder*, pp. 31-32.
3. Hugh Nibley, *No Ma'am, That's Not History*, p. 45.
4. Op. cit., p. 31.
5. Matthew 28:20.
6. Mark E. Petersen, *Which Church is Right?*, p. 7.
7. Talmage, *The Great Apostasy*, p. 97.

8. Eusebius, *History of the Church*, Book 4, 22.
9. Mark 4:34.
10. 2 Peter 3:16.
11. *History*, Book 4, 7.
12. *Heresies Answered*, Book 3.
13. Book 4, 21.
14. Book 3, 38.
15. Eusebius, Book 4, 22 (Italics mine).
16. p. 130.
17. Cited in Bettenson, *Documents of the Christian Church*, p. 68.
18. Ibid., p. 69.
19. Cited in Bettenson, ibid., p. 71.
20. Book 6, 43.
21. Book 7, 30.
22. Talmage, *The Great Apostasy*, p. 132. The first such synod was, of course, the Council of Jerusalem (Acts 15).
23. Matthew 16:18.
24. Mark 10:46-48.
25. Matthew 13:47-49.
26. *Lumen Gentium* 8.
27. Irving Wallace, *The Twenty-Seventh Wife*, quoted in M.C. Burrell, *Wide of the Truth*, p. 21.
28. *History*, Century 1, Vol. I, p. 317.
29. *History of the Church*, Vol. III, quoted in Brodie, op. cit., p. 208.
30. *Autobiography*, p. 421.
31. Gordon B. Hinckley, *Truth Restored*, pp. 78-9.
32. Op. cit., pp. 437-8.
33. Joseph Fielding Smith, *Essentials in Church History*, p. 171.
34. Ibid., p. 167.
35. Biographical note, Appendix I to Lucy Mack Smith's *History*. On the defections from the Quorum of the Twelve Apostles, see Roberts, p. 445, Fielding Smith, pp. 188-9, 199, 381 and footnote p. 360, and Brodie, pp. 319 and 163-5.
36. For a more detailed discussion of the splinter groups see Thomas F. O'Dea, *The Mormons*, pp. 70-72.

Chapter 8: Mormon Doctrine

1. Cyril Eastwood, *Life and Thought in the Ancient World*, p. 106.
2. Thomas F. O'Dea, *The Mormons*, p. 72.
3. *Why I Believe*, p. 95.
4. p. 73.
5. Talmage, *Articles of Faith*, p. 471.
6. Ibid., p. 472.
7. Quoted in Fraser, *Is Mormonism Christian?* pp. 44 and 59. The Reorganized Church rejects Young's teaching.
8. Talmage, op. cit., p. 472.
9. John 1:1-15.
10. Op. cit., p. 92.

11. Op. cit., p. 39.
12. *A Marvelous Work and a Wonder,* p. 18.
13. Ibid., p. 14.
14. Op. cit., p. 40.
15. *Articles of Faith,* p. 529.
16. Ibid.
17. Matthew 28:19.
18. Op. cit., pp. 108-9.
19. Ibid., pp. 104-5.
20. Talmage, op. cit., p. 122.
21. The point is developed at length by Dr John Marsh on p. 117 of his *Pelican Commentary on St John's Gospel.*
22. Acts 18:24-6.
23. See Mosiah 16:11 and Helaman 12:25-26.
24. *Doctrine and Covenants* 131:1-4. Richards, op. cit., p. 195.
25. Richards, p. 196.
26. *Doctrine and Covenants* 132:19-21.
27. Talmage, op. cit., pp. 442-3.
28. Op. cit., p. 195.
29. *Journal of Discourses,* Vol. II, pp. 81-2; quoted in Fraser, *Is Mormonism Christian?,* p. 62.
30. Ibid., Vol. IV, p. 210; quoted in Fraser, p. 63.
31. Matthew 22:23-31; Mark 12:18-26; Luke 20:27-37.
32. Matthew 22:29-31.
33. Maurice C. Burrell, *Wide of the Truth,* p. 127.
34. Fraser, *Is Mormonism Christian?* p. 29.

Bibliography

The following works are accepted by Mormons as having equal authority with the Bible.

Book of Mormon, Salt Lake Edition, 1920.
Doctrine and Covenants, Salt Lake City, Utah, 1973.
Pearl of Great Price, Salt Lake City, Utah, 1973.

General

Fawn M. Brodie, *No Man Knows My History: The Life of Joseph Smith, the Mormon Prophet*, Alfred A. Knopf Inc., 1945, and Eyre and Spottiswoode Ltd, 1963. Thoroughly documented. Indispensable to a study of Mormonism.

Maurice C. Burrell, *Wide of the Truth*, Marshall, Morgan and Scott, 1972.

Maurice C. Burrell and J. Stafford Wright, *Some Modern Faiths*, Inter-Varsity Press, 1973, 1974.

George Edward Clark, *Why I Believe: Fifty-Four Evidences of the Divine Calling of Joseph Smith*, Bookcraft, Salt Lake City, 1952.

Anthony A. Hoekema, *The Four Major Cults*, The Paternoster Press, 1963, 1972.

W.R. Martin, *The Maze of Mormonism*, Marshall, Morgan and Scott, 1962, 1963.

Thomas F. O'Dea, *The Mormons*, The University of Chicago Press, 1957.

LeGrand Richards, *A Marvelous Work and a Wonder*, Deseret Enterprises Ltd, 1969.

L. Rumble, *The Mormons*, The Catholic Truth Society, 1958.

James E. Talmage, *Articles of Faith*, London: The Church of Jesus Christ of Latter-Day Saints, West European Mission, 1962.

Chapters 1 and 2

James Black, *New Forms of the Old Faith* (Baird Lecture, 1946-47), Thomas Nelson and Sons Ltd.

Fawn M. Brodie, *No Man Knows My History.*

Gordon B. Hinckley, *Truth Restored: A short History of the Church of Jesus Christ of Latter-day Saints,* Deseret News Press, 1947, 1969.

W.R. Martin, *The Maze of Mormonism.*

Hugh Nibley, *No Ma'am, That's Not History,* Bookcraft, 1946, 1974. The Mormon reply to Brodie's biography of Joseph Smith.

Thomas F. O'Dea, *The Mormons.*

LeGrand Richards, *A Marvelous Work and a Wonder.*

B.H. Roberts, *A Comprehensive History of the Church of Jesus Christ of Latter-day Saints,* Century One, Vol. 1, Brigham Young University Press, 1957, 1976.

J. Oswald Sanders, *Heresies Ancient and Modern,* Marshall, Morgan and Scott, Ltd, 1948.

Joseph Fielding Smith, *Essentials in Church History,* Deseret Book Company, 1950, 1979.

Lucy Mack Smith, *History of Joseph Smith the Prophet by His Mother,* Ed. Preston Nibley, Bookcraft, 1958.

Chapters 3, 4 and 5

G.H.S. Bushnell, *The First Americans: The Pre-Columbian Civilisations,* Thames and Hudson, 1968.

G.H.S. Bushnell, *Ancient Arts of the Americas,* Thames and Hudson, 1965.

George Edward Clark, *Why I Believe.*

Michael D. Coe, *The Maya,* Thames and Hudson, 1966.

Michael D. Coe, *Mexico,* London: Thames and Hudson.

Glyn Daniel, *The First Civilisations,* Penguin Books, 1971.

C. Dawson, *Progress and Religion,* Sheed and Ward, 1929, 1938.

Thomas Stuart Ferguson, *One Fold and One Shepherd,* Books of California, 1958.

E.W. Heaton, *Everyday Life in Old Testament Times,* B.T. Batsford Ltd, 1956, 1966.

Milton R. Hunter, *Archaeology and the Book of Mormon,* Deseret Book Co., 1969.

Milton R. Hunter, *Christ in Ancient America,* Deseret Book Co., 1972.

Milton R. Hunter and Thomas Stuart Ferguson, *Ancient America and the Book of Mormon,* Kolob Book Company, 1950, 1957.

Alvin M. Josephy Jnr, *The Indian Heritage of America,* London: Penguin Books, 1968, 1975.

W.R. Martin, *The Maze of Mormonism.*

B.H. Roberts, *History.*

James E. Talmage, *Articles of Faith.*

Ruth Murray Underhill, *Red Man's America: A History of Indians in the United States,* University of Chicago Press, 1953.

Robert Wauchope, *Lost Tribes and Sunken Continents: Myth and Method in the Study of American Indians,* University of Chicago Press, 1962, 1970.

Robert Wauchope, General Editor, *Handbook of Middle American Indians,* Vol. 1: *Natural Environment and Early Cultures,* Volume Editor, Robert C. West, Texas: University of Texas Press, 1964.

Encyclopedia Americana

Encyclopaedia Britannica, 1969 Edition.

Chapter 6

George Edward Clark, *Why I Believe.*

Stanley Cook, *An Introduction to the Bible,* Penguin Books, 1945.

Albert Gélin, *The Religion of Israel,* Burns and Oates, 1959.

E.W. Heaton, *The Old Testament Prophets,* London: Penguin Books, 1958, 1964.

Anthony A. Hoekema, *The Four Major Cults.*

W.R. Martin, *The Maze of Mormonism.*

William Neil, *One-Volume Bible Commentary,* Hodder and Stoughton, 1962, 1973.

B.H. Roberts, *History.*

James E. Talmage, *Articles of Faith.*

Chapter 7

Walter M. Abbott, SJ, General Editor, *The Documents of Vatican II,* Geoffrey Chapman, 1965, 1967.

Henry Bettenson Ed., *Documents of the Christian Church,* Oxford University Press, 1963, 1967.

Fawn M. Brodie, *No Man Knows My History.*

M.C. Burrell, *Wide of the Truth.*

Henry Chadwick, *The Early Church,* Penguin Books, 1967, 1974.

Jean Danielou and Henri Marrou, *The Christian Centuries I: The First Six Hundred Years,* Darton, Longman and Todd, 1964

Eusebius, *The History of the Church,* Trans. G.A.Williamson, Penguin Books, 1965, 1967

Thomas F. O'Dea, *The Mormons*

Hugh Nibley, *No Ma'am, That's Not History*

Gordon B. Hinckley, *Truth Restored*

Mark E. Petersen, *Which Church is Right?* The British Mission

Parley P. Pratt, *Autobiography*, The Deseret Book Co., 1938, 1975
LeGrand Richards, *A Marvelous Work and a Wonder*
B.H. Roberts, *History*
Joseph Fielding Smith, *Essentials in Church History*
Lucy Mack Smith, *History*
James E. Talmage, *Articles of Faith*
James E. Talmage, *The Great Apostasy*, Deseret Enterprises Ltd,
    1909

Chapter 8

Maurice C. Burrell and J. Stafford Wright, *Some Modern Faiths*,
    chapter 3
George Edward Clark, *Why I Believe*
Cyril C. Eastwood, *Life and Thought in the Ancient World*, Peter
    Smith Ltd, 1964
Gordon H. Fraser, *Is Mormonism Christian?* The Moody Press,
    1957, 1965
John Marsh, *Pelican Commentary on St John's Gospel*, Penguin
    Books, 1968, 1971
Thomas F. O'Dea, *The Mormons*
LeGrand Richards, *A Marvelous Work and a Wonder*
L. Rumble, *The Mormons*, The Catholic Truth Society, 1958
James E. Talmage, *Articles of Faith*